The Grace of Waiting

MARGARET WHIPP

The Grace of Waiting

CANTERBURY
PRESS
Norwich

© Margaret Whipp 2017

First published in 2017 by the Canterbury Press Norwich
Editorial office
3rd Floor, Invicta House
108–114 Golden Lane
London EC1Y 0TG, UK
www.canterburypress.co.uk

Canterbury Press is an imprint of Hymns Ancient & Modern Ltd
(a registered charity)

Hymns Ancient & Modern® is a registered trademark of
Hymns Ancient & Modern Ltd
13A Hellesdon Park Road, Norwich,
Norfolk NR6 5DR, UK

British Library Cataloguing in Publication data

A catalogue record for this book is available
from the British Library

978 1 84825 977 5

Typeset by Manila Typesetting Company
Printed and bound in Great Britain by
CPI Group (UK) Ltd

Contents

Introduction

If there is a book you want to read, but it hasn't been written yet, then you must write it. (Toni Morrison)[1]

People tell me every day how much they hate waiting. They have tried to be patient. They have tried not to show how anxious and fretful and frustrated they feel about their situation. They have struggled to accept not knowing how long they may be kept waiting; they have done their best to embrace not being in control of the outcome of their waiting; but still, as their waiting drags on, they find it hard to be graceful about it.

'I'm writing a book about waiting,' I venture, with a wry smile. And then I wait for a response.

This book is the fruit of hundreds of everyday conversations with people who are trying to be patient.[2] Many of them make light of their struggles. 'I guess that's why we're called "patients"!' Others unleash a torrent of pent-up fears and resentment. 'They never tell you anything.' 'It's ridiculous.' 'It's about time they sorted this system out.' 'I can't believe it has to take this long.' Some honest souls are more reflective about their waiting. 'The hard thing is the uncertainty.' 'I'm so worried.' 'I don't know what this will mean for the family.'

After the harrumphing, the sighs. After the sighs, the tears. After the tears, a few more wry smiles. And then, perhaps, the real conversation can begin.

As a hospital chaplain, I recognize how isolated people become in their waiting. They feel left out and forgotten, anxious that life is passing them by. One of the greatest comforts is having someone to talk to, someone who can share the waiting and reassure them that they have not been totally abandoned. It's surprising how much a simple greeting can do to lighten a dark hour, bringing a glimmer of quiet grace.

As I come alongside others in their waiting, I try to be, in Kafka's gentle phrase, 'a true attendant upon grace'. Our brief time together may, or may not, unfold into a profound exchange of wisdom and compassion; but I try to remain patient and quietly openhearted, however seemingly fruitless my efforts appear. The hidden grace of waiting is not mine to command. 'Perhaps it will come; perhaps it will not come. Perhaps this quiet yet unquiet waiting is the harbinger of grace, or perhaps it is grace itself' (Janouch, p. 166).

These 'quiet yet unquiet' glimpses of grace are the subject of this book. They are glimpses of what patience feels like, how we learn and practise it, and the unlikely gifts that it brings.

Many of these insights have been gleaned from my years of pastoral experience of slowly waiting with others, especially in hospital contexts. Most have found resonances in the dark waiting times of my own personal experience. None of them, I hope, are trite or untested. This will not be a book, therefore, of exhortation or theory. It is more of a pilgrim's travel guide, sketched out for the benefit of those who will follow the same rough pathways, seeking a fellow-pilgrim's encouragement for the road ahead.

I am grateful, more than I can say, to all those who have, knowingly or unknowingly, contributed to this book. They are friends who have patiently walked with me through some blistering and treacherous paths of life, and strangers whom I have come alongside for shorter or longer stretches along their way. Falling into step with one another, and sharing our stories of unchosen waiting and incomprehensible delays, we have grown more patient with ourselves, and more appreciative of the necessary slowness of our unique pilgrimages through life. Friends and strangers alike, their wisdom and experience and, above all, their patience has returned to mind throughout the writing of this book. In their wise ways and kindly words, they have helped me to appreciate the sheer grace of waiting, to practise the unfashionable virtue of patience, and to embrace its surprising and beautiful gifts.

To all these fellow-pilgrims in patience, with respect and affection, I dedicate this book.

Notes

1 Tweet 30 October 2013.
2 To preserve anonymity, names and details have been changed throughout the book.

I

The Waiting Room

How long, O Lord? (Psalm 13.1)

Shirley is sitting alone in the crowded waiting room. Fingers restless, shoulders tight, chin upturned, her eyes constantly scan the double doors where nurses come and go. For what seems like an eternity, Shirley waits for her appointment, wondering how long it will be before somebody calls her name. Meanwhile, everything in her struggles to contain the dread anguish of waiting. How long?

These hours spent in the waiting rooms of life are rarely pleasant, and, for the most part, unavoidable. It can be terribly hard to wait. We would rather push things quickly along, anxious to spare ourselves the uncertainty and helplessness of waiting. Yet waiting is a fundamental human and social reality. Life is full of unchosen, unwanted waiting – in times of change and transition, in sickness and recovery, in parenting and caring, in old age and incapacity, in dying and grieving, and in the countless ordinary delays and disruptions of daily life.

This book is a personal, spiritual and practical exploration of necessary waiting – and it has taken time, and patience, to write.

Waiting times

I work within an NHS Hospital Trust where nobody likes to wait. There are systems in place to monitor waiting times at every opportunity. When someone attends a clinic, we measure the minutes spent waiting for their appointment. When they come to the emergency department, we measure the hours it takes for them to see a nurse or doctor. If they have cancer, or need surgery for an arthritic hip, we measure the days and weeks they are kept wait-ing before diagnostic tests or active treatment can begin. We have targets to meet and statistics to report. The overriding goal is to reduce or eliminate the time spent waiting for active care.

History will judge us to be an impatient generation. We are in such a rush, so much of the time, unforgiving in our haste. We have come to see waiting as nothing more than a problem, a nuisance, an interruption in the stream of life, an irritating pause button that breaks the illusion of cheerful continuity and control. The idea that waiting is often necessary, or occasionally valuable, seems hopelessly old-fashioned and unpopular.

Yet what I have learned, as a painstaking observer in countless waiting rooms of life, both literal and metaphorical, is that a time of waiting that is actively embraced, and not breezily rejected, can become an opportunity for surprising spiritual growth and existential discovery.

My personal interest in waiting dates back to the years I spent in medical practice. I was a young woman, working as a consultant oncologist in the local cancer hospital. Perhaps, in my own way, I was also waiting to grow up, absorbing essential life lessons from the many older people who were patients in my care. Immersed in other people's suffering and fears, I was impressed by the wisdom and resilience in many of those who attended my clinics. Most of them were unsophisticated people, navigating their path through life without any substantial academic or professional expertise. They were not well versed in either medical or theological learn-ing. Yet as I watched people wrestling tragedy and raw fear, I marvelled at the spiritual resources that so often sustained them. It was a kind of grace.

It was during those years that I came across a charcoal sketch, simply entitled *The Waiting Room*. It was no great work of art, but I found it surprisingly moving. It had been commissioned by a breast cancer charity that was trying to portray aspects of what it meant to live with a life-threatening disease. Something about the artist's sketch resonated very keenly with my daily clinical expe-rience of looking out on a room full of waiting patients. Every face shown by the artist captured something unique, and intense, about this human reality of waiting. The tautness of expression, the different shades of frustration, endurance, distraction and hope – played out on a dozen or so faces – each hinting at some hidden inside story of what it meant, personally and phenomenologically, to wait.

The brutal honesty of this sketch touched something deeply human for me. We spend so much of our lives waiting, not only when we are sick, but in all kinds of everyday circumstances. Waiting for the lights to change. Waiting for the weather to improve. Waiting for exam results. Waiting for love. Waiting for the computer to reboot. Waiting for a ceasefire. Waiting for a holiday. Waiting for a creative idea. Waiting for a baby. However mundane or mysterious, there is always something we are anticipating on the horizon.

Waiting, like nothing else, reveals our complex human relationship with time. We have some desire, some goal in mind; it may not seem too far away, yet still we must wait for the possibility to come into focus, for the actuality to come within reach. We cannot rush to grasp the future with any certainty. We cannot force the pace of life's unavoidable slowness. Time will not let us do that. Some things simply have to unfold. And so, we are constrained to wait.

As a hospital chaplain, I am often called to come alongside people in their waiting. Unlike our hospital managers, or the politicians who commission their services, it is not my job to home in on quantitative targets to reduce their waiting time. And, unlike my clinical colleagues, it is not my responsibility to progress their diagnosis or to initiate treatment. My role is more patient and personal, more attentive and watchful, with an eye not for the quantitative reduction of waiting but for its qualitative depth and meaning and potential value. My ministry is to sustain and support the waiting soul, the person grappling with the anguish and uncertainties of temporal existence, and to chart together some path of 'graceful waiting'.

This book is written in the belief that, ultimately, all our waiting is waiting on God. Perhaps, even more importantly, in our waiting we might glimpse how God is somehow waiting for us. What I hope to explore in the coming pages is the potential strength and meaning that comes through patience. Is it possible to learn to wait, not resentfully, but peacefully and patiently? Is there a grace in the waiting?

From time to time down the years I have been intrigued to meet people who seem to have embraced just this possibility. I remember speaking with a remarkable young minister while queuing for the refectory at a conference. He told me that some years earlier he had decided that, whenever he went shopping at the supermarket, he would deliberately choose the longest check-out queue. Instead of huffing and puffing about the precious time he was wasting through having to wait his turn for the till, my friend embraced this small, but immensely telling, spiritual discipline of gathering up the necessary peace and patience to learn to wait. It was his act of unforced, quiet obedience: a silent witness against the restless hurry that generates so much unnecessary pain and tension in modern life.

Of course, it is not nearly so easy when something more serious is at stake. Yet perhaps, as we learn to practise waiting in the small inconveniences of daily life, we may be readier to face the challenges of more fearful times of terrible tension and dread.

The poet Julia Darling, who died in 2005, put her own experiences of waiting to good effect. She decided to write about her treatment for breast cancer and her time spent in hospital. In a series of gently ironic poems, she pioneered fresh ways of engaging illness through the sheer communicative power of her pen. Her vignettes are so accurate and full of compassionate detail that they have the effect of soothing and transforming some of the appalling challenges of a frightening illness and a harsh prognosis.

One of my favourite poems from her collection describes 'A Waiting Room in August'. With exquisite detail, Darling conjures up the tension and dignity of patients waiting 'like a drum' for the coming summons. The profound struggle of waiting is captured by the contrast between a deep-felt inner anxiety and a proudly maintained outer decorum of those, with hands folded, shoes polished and wigs lying 'patiently' on dignified heads, have 'made an art of it'. The poem ends with the comic-exasperated cry: 'Haven't we waited beautifully?' (Darling, p. 20).

Like it or not, Darling appreciates that the reality of waiting cannot be side-stepped or obliterated; somehow it has to be borne. Sweetly and oh-so-subtly, the poem puts the question as to whether and how we might 'make an art of it'. This book is part of my attempt, as a Christian, to wrest some unfashionable blessings from these perennial human challenges of waiting, and to see if the time-honoured art and practice of patience can guide us along the way.

The relentless march of activity

The problem with waiting is that it runs counter to our cultural expectations of ceaseless activity. Our anxiety, as busy modern individuals, is not simply that we feel helpless when we are forced to wait. We face a deeper problem, because we judge that waiting is a useless and insulting waste of our precious time. What is the point of waiting when we ought to be getting on with life? Even children pick up this joyless contemporary impatience: as a petulant toddler complains on a popular comic video, 'Hurry up, lady, I have things to DOOO!'

This relentless, driven attitude towards time is a peculiarly modern obsession. We suffer from chronic busyness, anxious and greedy in our relationship with the passage of time. Many of us, not only in public but also in the private chambers of the mind, are caught in the acceleration traps of a 24/7 society with its ever-increasing frenetic pace of innovation, connectivity and expectation. Perhaps the truth is that we are frightened to slow down in case we fall behind.

This insatiable activism is one of the most serious spiritual dystopias of contemporary life. We are addicted to keeping 'busy'. Our everyday conversation betrays an alarming set of values where being 'busy' is regarded as socially admirable – a kind of boast, even when it is disguised as a complaint. Whenever a colleague asks if I am 'busy' at work, it's hard to resist the pretty strong expectation of a positive reply. Typically, our conversation will go back and forth in mildly competitive terms, amid friendly sighs and grins, as my colleague and I exchange subtly self-promoting and self-pitying updates on the manic pace of activity that we are each respectively trying to sustain.

Recently, I experimented with a different script. In response to the question, 'Are you busy?', I tried a quiet pause. Instead of rushing to affirm my self-importance with the usual catalogue of ceaseless demands queuing up for my attention, I would venture a more reflective answer along the lines that chaplains try to avoid unthinking busyness. The result has been some fascinating, and rather moving, conversations with colleagues who would dearly love to break free from the merciless trap of escalating hyper-activism.

Stephen Cherry, the Dean of King's College Cambridge, identifies this uncritical busyness as one of the most damaging moral distortions of our age. Intriguingly, he puts this on a par with the ancient deadly sin of sloth. Chronic busyness, he maintains, should be seen as more of a vice than a virtue, because it conspires to deaden our moral and spiritual sensitivities to the true value and purpose of God-given time. Cherry believes that Christians should be among the first to challenge a prevailing culture of toxic busyness, on the grounds that busyness:

- distorts your perception
- makes you feel self-important
- makes you rude
- is an excuse for impatience
- is an excuse for not getting things done
- is addictive
- burns you out
- is lazy – chronic busyness occurs when you have not asked the important questions or decided on your priorities (Cherry, 2012).

Mindless busyness is a cruel and all-pervasive trap in our society. And if I am caught in this habitual hyper-active mindset, it is little wonder that waiting comes to feel so alien and oppressive. Having to wait, more than any other experience, challenges the fond illusion that my timetable, my activism, my busy plans for getting things done, should take priority over everybody and everything else that matters.

All in good time

From the first poetic words of the book of Genesis, the Bible offers a graceful and counter-cultural perspective on time. In the beautiful story of creation, we read about the shaping of a whole universe, morning by morning and evening by evening – all proceeding in God's good time. In contrast to the prevailing commercialization of time, which grasps each unforgiving minute for some instrumental advantage, we sense an all-encompassing spiritual wisdom that values the mystery of time, from its first inception, as a gift of pure grace. This perspective is essential if we are to embrace the challenge of faithful waiting.

Taking an eternal perspective, we might begin to reframe the temporal meaning and necessity of waiting. In God's good time, we intuit a deeper value in our times of waiting, more as a welcome shadow side to human activity, and less a disruptive intrusion into our anticipated plans. From this contemplative perspective, we might cultivate a more holistic understanding of time's rich ecology, within which our seasons of waiting find their necessary depth and purpose. Having to wait for something, from this standpoint, is not so much like coming up against a roadblock or structural fault in the smooth onward progress of 'our' time. Instead we begin to glimpse something of a larger providence, gently inviting our fitful human priorities to bend in service to an eternal weight of glory.

My hope for this book is to gently foster this graceful and more kindly approach to waiting. I came to the topic as a priest and pastor, drawn by a mysterious sense that in all our human waiting there is some hidden invitation to wait on God's grace.

I cannot claim that this has been an easy book to write. It has presented me, at every stage, with a personal challenge to probe the dark matter of our human fears and longings, and to begin to chart this strange territory of time and eternity that is so singularly compressed in the experience of waiting. I have had to reflect very deeply on my own relationship to time, and to ask searching questions of my taken-for-granted understandings of providence and the pace of human events. Not surprisingly, I have been forced to 'wait' through a prolonged gestation before I could feel ready to give birth to my ideas.

My research for this book has inched forward slowly and tentatively. I am grateful for those friends and fellow-travellers who have shared their honest struggles and revealed their own modest, but hard-earned, wisdom – one conversation at a time. Little by little, I have sensed faint outlines emerging from the mists of waiting – a luminous phrase here, a glowing prayer there – like so many points of light shining amid the darkness. Like Jacob (Genesis 32.22–31), I have wrestled both the unbearable intensity of waiting, along with what I can only call the angelic sweetness of waiting: slowly, patiently and on my knees.

This gradual and gracious process has shaped not only the content but also the style of the book. It is not a textbook, or moral and theological treatise on the 'meaning in the waiting', but rather a personal and spiritual invitation to live and pray gracefully in the midst of each unexpected and unchosen hiatus along the path of life. I hope it will bring sustenance in your own struggles.

Kindly wait

There is a helpful distinction between two different Greek words for 'time'. The word *chronos* describes the continuing passage of time. It is the root for our word 'chronology', the regular, moving time that can be measured by a clock. A rather different meaning is captured by the word *kairos*, which suggests an opportune time. I think of the kairos moment as a point of intersection between time and eternity – which emerges all in good time – whenever we glimpse the grace of God coming more fully into focus within the protracted uncertainties of our ongoing life.

For every movement of the spirit there is a due season. A friend who had struggled for years with a restless sense of vocation described his longing for a sense of direction to become clear. In his fretful waiting, he recalled the wisdom he had learned from walking with his father's old pocket compass. His father had taught him that when we are trying to map a way forward, we have to wait for the compass needle to settle. This delicately balanced instrument swings and wavers for some time before it settles to the steady pull of the north. This became a lifelong lesson for my friend. Despite the anguish of waiting, he realized that there was nothing to be gained, and a great deal potentially to lose, by rushing onward before the time for action had become fully clear.

You may be approaching this book in the hope of finding some resolution to some particular challenge of waiting. Perhaps someone has suggested that you read a book instead of fussing and fretting about the uncertainties you face. If that is the case, then I hope that the book will not disappoint you. It is not my intention to offer any kind of escape or solution to the perennial problem of waiting, which is nothing more nor less than an ineradicable part of our life as creatures in time.

What I hope this book will foster is a patient and graceful perspective that will deepen and sustain your spiritual capacity for skilful waiting. I doubt you will gain much by skipping through its pages in a hurry. Whether you have picked up the book in the teeth of a challenging time for yourself or someone close to you, or whether you have decided to read about waiting as a calmer spiritual exercise – perhaps for the season of Advent or Lent – I would urge you to embrace the spirit of this book in practice, and not merely in theory.

Each chapter will introduce different themes and experiences, like so many classrooms in the school of patience. Take your time. Let yourself walk slowly through the ideas explored in each chapter, allowing time to pray and ponder over those questions that resonate most deeply with your experience. You may need to pause over a line of poetry or a verse of scripture, or to rest in quiet meditation wherever you sense God's gracious questioning of your ingrained thoughts and habits of the heart.

At the end of each chapter you will find a simple spiritual exercise, or practicum. As the name suggests, the challenge of waiting presents a very practical opportunity for us to grow in the grace of patience. These exercises are not meant to be rushed through as an optional postscript to some more substantial intellectual message. Since waiting is a very practical matter, which involves us both physically and spiritually, and unavoidably temporally, then you will need to give the time for your soul and body to internalize and truly embrace some of the holy wisdom that you are hoping to cultivate.

Practicum – time out for a simple body prayer

This is an exercise adapted from Father Richard Rohr (2014). You will need to find space and time, perhaps at the end or the beginning of the day, to make this fourfold prayer of waiting in a graceful and expectant way.

AWAIT – Sit or kneel, with your hands palm up, in a gesture of receptivity. Await God's presence. Give time to wait, not as you expect or hope or imagine God's presence to feel, but just as it is in this moment of time.

ALLOW – Reach up, with your hands open to this encounter. Let go your cherished sense of control. Allow a sense of God's presence (or God's holy absence) to come and be what it is, without meeting your preferences and expectations.

ACCEPT – Bring your hands, cupped towards the place of the heart. Accept as a gift whatever is real in this moment of prayer. Whatever does or does not come to you, accept that you are not in charge. Accept the infinity and transcendence of God's presence, which is real and present whether or not you have any awareness.

ATTEND – Finally stretch out your hands, in a gesture of readiness and response. Make an active gift of your waiting, as you attend to what you are called to, whatever reorientation or recommitment God now invites.

For God alone my soul waits in silence. (Psalm 62.5)

2

Practice Time

Love is patient. (1 Corinthians 13.4)

I watched at first with amusement, and then with admiring awe, as the young mother outside my neighbour's house tried to settle an elderly in-law, plus two children under five, into their car seats, at the same time as packing their Christmas presents, toys, bags, buggies – and a visiting poodle – into the rear luggage compartment.

'Where's Fluffy?' wailed the younger infant. 'I want my juice in here!' commanded the older of the two, wriggling like an out-of-control octopus. Somehow the mother managed to collapse the buggy and contain the poodle before the younger child started hitting the older, and fresh pandemonium broke out on the back seat. All this was before the fifty-mile journey back home, where she would have to repeat the whole procedure in reverse.

Everyday life provides ample opportunities for practising patience. But patience is not always easy to practise when we are faced with the dismal reality of waiting.

Why are we waiting?

Frustrated football fans take up the chant with great gusto when their team fails to pick up the pace and move the game along in the right direction. Whining children, equally, learn precisely how to wind up their elders with vocal protests about the slowness of events. 'Are we nearly there yet?' 'Why are we waiting?'

Whenever events fail to move forward in line with our personal satisfaction, it is natural enough to demand 'Why?' Children in our culture learn the trick of asking 'Why?' at a very early age.

But it is a question that scarcely cuts to the root of our irritation and sense of personal impotence. Whenever our personal quality of life has been disrupted by some necessary delay, we may look for some kind of satisfaction in demanding answers to the question 'Why?' But the annoying fact remains that no human being, child or adult, can ever be fully in control of every situation in their lives.

The stubborn fact remains that, sometimes in life, we will have no alternative but to wait, sometimes for a long time, and with no ready explanation. This is not to argue that all waiting is either necessary or inevitable. There is a time to act as well as a time to wait: and very important it is to know the difference. It would be unkind and unfair to encourage compliant passivity in the face of every unjust or unreasonable delay.

My focus in this book, however, is not on the waiting that can be circumvented or eliminated from our lives. We have plenty of encouragement, in our consumerist culture, to assert our rights and make our demands felt when we are forced to wait because of other people's carelessness or incompetence. What concerns me primarily, as a pastoral and profoundly spiritual issue, is the ineradicable waiting that cannot be blamed on any individual or system, but that is simply an intrinsic part of our human experience in time.

We have to wait for our own bodies: as children, we have to wait to grow bigger and stronger; as young people, we have to wait to develop sexually and emotionally, and to grow in confidence and ability; later in life we will have to wait on our own frailty, probably with increasing dependence on others; and the time will come, sooner or later, when we are waiting for our death. Waiting is part of our human condition.

Throughout our lives, we have to wait for other people. Their needs, their priorities, their actions and inactions, near or far, justified or unjustified, will impact on us. The frailty of others or the frustration of 'events' will constrain my precious liberty; and then no amount of loud protest and misplaced indignation will assuage my fundamental discomfort. Waiting is part of our social situation. My time frame does not rule the universe. It takes patience to flow graciously between competing time frames, to bear compassionately with the needs and schedules of others, and to live peacefully on a planet that revolves through cycles of eonic time, with no special consideration for the petty preferences of my mortal existence.

In the subsequent chapters of this book, I shall be reflecting on some of the most challenging waiting times in life. We shall be accompanying people who are waiting for serious results and outcomes, waiting anxiously for birth, or wearily for death. Perhaps a more mature alternative to our insistent, and finally unsatisfying, 'Why?' questions would be some broader reflection on the 'How?' and the 'What?' of waiting. What is the real purpose of waiting? And what is ultimately worth waiting for? Who is waiting with us, or for us? What are the skills of waiting? How could we learn to wait peacefully, kindly? What grace and meaning might we discover in our waiting? These are positive spiritual and psychological questions, rather than mere whingeing protests: and they lead us in the direction of a deliberate cultivation of the graceful virtue of patience.

Patience is a virtue

There is a wrong kind of patience which sometimes masquerades as Christian virtue. Lazy acquiescence with bullying and injustice is not patience. Resignation in the face of a weakness that could be overcome with effort and perseverance is not patience. Passivity and inaction that fails to engage lovingly with the complexities of the world is not patience. Apathy and boredom, displacement and collusion, are not patience: they are forms of evasion, and spiritual, as well as moral, immaturity.

Josef Pieper inveighs against these common misunderstandings, when he states that patience does not mean 'an indiscriminate, self-immolating, crabbed, joyless and spineless submission to whatever evil is met with' (Pieper, p. 129). By contrast, authentically Christian patience actively unites our hearts with the infinitely patient God in a positive attitude of humble gratitude and free compassion.

We can learn to be patient. It is a matter of acquired disposition and intentional character formation: nobody is born with patience. Think of a hungry infant, wailing and clamouring for the immediate satisfaction of their primal needs. Human beings, like all other animals, possess fundamental drives for survival that make them inherently, or we might say biologically, impatient. The delayed gratification of basic needs, especially for dependent infants, could be a serious threat to their continuing existence. No wonder, then, that even in adults the experience of waiting can provoke such acutely uncomfortable feelings – of helplessness, infantile rage or despair.

Learning patience, therefore, can be quite a struggle. The deliberate choice to cultivate moral and spiritual maturity is the business of what we sometimes call ascetical practice. The classic ascetical tradition, with its determination to combat instinctive self-centredness, has not always had a good press in Christian history. We have learned to be suspicious of those stereotypically joyless disciplines and deprivations that are little more than religiously legitimated masochism. But there is an opposite danger, for a morally soft generation, which is to give in to childish self-gratification by never engaging with any serious struggle for genuinely adult virtue and happiness.

I have learned from our ascetic tradition that the sacred art of waiting depends on two fundamental insights into human maturation. The first is that any worthwhile skill, whether physical or spiritual, can be developed through practice – that is the intentional, persistent exercise of a way of living in the world – and this applies to the learned exercise of human patience. The second is that the value and meaning of patience can only fully be grasped in the light of self-transcending relationships. Put more simply, I believe that all human patience is ultimately a practice of waiting on God.

These two principles of ascetical theology will shape the agenda for all that follows in this book, as I seek to expand and reimagine the possibilities and practices of graceful waiting. But first, I must ask the reader to wait a little, and bear patiently with my unfolding agenda. Before we consider the positive questions about the cultivation of Christian patience, we need to clear the ground by enquiring about the tragically damaging loss of patience in our hypermodern world.

Losing patience

Patience used to be greatly admired. It is sobering and rather curious to realize that the eclipse of patience, as a core virtue, represents a very recent and modern shift in human sensibilities. Steadfastness of character, the endurance of difficulty and the capacity of forbearance under provocation were qualities highly regarded in the ancient world. Stoics in particular, while stressing the unity of all the virtues, often singled out patience as one of the supreme qualities of the disciplined and dispassionate soul.

Early Christian theologians similarly preached with great warmth on the theme of patience, extending beyond the cool self-mastery of the Stoics through their profoundly personal identification with the inspiring patience of God in Christ. Writing in the third century 'on the advantage of patience', Cyprian of Carthage wrote very tenderly of the way in which Christ bore with suffering. 'The Word of God is led silently to the slaughter.' 'He speaks not, nor is moved, nor declares His majesty even in His very passion itself . . . in order that in Christ a full and perfect patience may be consummated' (Cyprian, p. 486).

For Tertullian, patience of soul and body was the highest and crowning Christian virtue. By contrast, every human sin could trace its roots down to an essential impatience with God. Augustine of Hippo held a similar regard for patience, arguing that every petition bar one in the Lord's Prayer is an appeal for the grace of Christian perseverance (Harned, pp. 55–6). When the list of seven heavenly virtues was promoted in the fifth century as an antidote to the seven deadly sins, the great quality of patience was extolled as one of its central elements.

In classic Christian theology, an ability to wait patiently was built on solid confidence in the promises of God. The Christian vision of time stretches out from the mundane experience of a flawed and sinful world to an eternal vision of fulfilment beyond time. Christians are called, in the power of God's Spirit, to live in the tension 'between the times' and to wait in hope for the final consummation of all things in Christ. This strong narrative of 'God's time' casts waiting as 'a necessary bridge between the temporal and eternal', with patience as an indispensable virtue for the realization of God's ultimate purposes (Robinson, p. 32).

In more recent times, however, even within Christian awareness, the value of patience among the virtues has been relegated to the sidelines. David Baily Harned, in a rare twentieth-century monograph on patience, observed that the leading dictionary of Christian ethics published in the western world contained no entry whatsoever on the virtue of patience.[1] In a careful historical study he traces the displacement of patience back to the nineteenth century. This key virtue, which was once regarded as indispensable for the realization of any strength of character, is seen in contemporary culture as morally outmoded, or else airily dismissed as a form of tractability reserved for the frail elderly and children. What is left of a once rich concept is now little more than a caricature. The very idea of patience has come to be equated with passivity and submission: a disposition that one might wish to impose on unruly youngsters, but not something that would be attractive to adults in search of the good life.

Reading back through far-reaching cultural and political upheavals in modern European history, Harned traces some of the factors that conspired to drive the virtue of patience out of fashion. The Communist Manifesto of 1848 cemented a critical social mindset that represents patience as 'a notion devised by oppressors to contain the restlessness and discontent of the oppressed' (Harned, p. 2). A growing sense of progress, not least in technology and the economy, similarly undermined traditional understandings of patience as anachronistic, reflecting a failure to assert and imagine the possibilities of radical social and personal transformation. 'Insofar as patience meant the uncomplaining endurance of adversity, it frequently seemed childlike in no very admirable sense' (Harned, p. 3). A robust impatience, especially with socially unjust structures, came to be promoted as the more admirable virtue for grown-ups.

Moving into the twentieth century, consumerist ideologies, often deliberately promoted by political economists, added further momentum to this cultured refusal of delayed gratification. Necessary waiting was no longer to be embraced as an opportunity for moral growth or spiritual development. Any requirement to wait was regarded, not as a healthy discipline, but rather as a miserly deprivation in an affluent society, which was claiming immediate gratification as a birthright. By the 1970s the era of instant financial credit found its perfect slogan in the bankers' strapline: 'Take the waiting out of wanting.' In our twenty-first century, the ubiquitous promotion of technological shortcuts and high-speed communication channels makes patient waiting seem foolishly redundant.

Taking a long view, we can see how the profound impatience of modern society is morally unprecedented in human cultural history. And while it would be churlish to discount the many blessings that have come from a healthy impatience with historic injustice and suffering, thoughtful Christians must seriously question the moral equation by which a proper exercise of patience is so little regarded that so many of our contemporaries find it excruciatingly hard to wait for anything.

Practice makes patience

Herein lies the challenge of this book. Our go-getting society regards waiting as undesirable, unwelcome and unprofitable. Little wonder, then, that the moral and dispositional skills of mature patience have fallen widely out of practice, and that occasions of necessary, or unexpected, waiting provoke such discomfort and outrage in our generation. We have either never learned, or we have somehow forgotten, what it means to practise patience.

Practice and patience go together. It takes practice to become patient; and the gift of patience equips us for every other kind of intentional practice throughout life.

Practice is the way that we develop any skill or attribute over a sustained period of time. In theological ethics, the importance of intentional practice has come to the fore in much recent reflection. Drawing on Alasdair MacIntyre's project on the ethics of virtue, moral philosophers understand that the practice of character strengths is key to many powerful human social and developmental dynamics. Within our Christian community, the exercise of certain practices will be inextricably linked with a distinctive way of thinking about life and living in God's world. Both the meaning and the doing of patience, therefore, as a spiritual practice, will be shaped by our understanding of what it means to know and experience the love of God in Jesus Christ and to live in hope of the fulfilment of God's promises.

This goes to the heart of our ascetical tradition as a school for character formation. Not only do Christians have a rationale and an inspiration for the practice of patience in our vision of fullness of life, but we are also blessed with a wealth of evocative images which flesh out the meaning of patience within our Christian narrative and community of spiritual and moral development. It is these graceful images that I hope to explore in more detail as a rich resource for our practice of patience. In later chapters of the book, we shall look in turn at these images of the wilderness, the winepress, the watch, the winter and the womb as rich metaphors for our seasons of waiting. My aim is, through an exploration of these dark and beautiful images, to come to a fuller understanding of what patience means, and to encourage the habitual exercise of practices of patience in the midst of our everyday lives.

Picturing patience

My computer screensaver is an image of Fra Angelico's famous fresco of the Annunciation. It always stops me in my tracks, pleading a moment's pause for holy waiting. How will I respond to the God who comes to me in time, who meets us in the 'now' of our lives? In this pregnant moment, what might it mean to say 'yes'?

How do we begin to envisage a truly adult and mature patience? In this book, I hope to delve into the phenomenology of waiting, to uncover what is distinctive about the virtue of patience from the perspective of Christian spirituality.

I have already noted that the apostolic fathers regarded patience as a primary virtue, the crowning disposition that gathered up all other virtues and dispositional strengths into a Christ-like whole. Patience was commended as the ultimate expression of waiting on God, a kind of negative capability that stretches our souls, and subjugates all our human agendas, to the measure of God's good timing. As T. S. Eliot prayerfully reflected, 'the faith and the love and the hope are all in the waiting' (Eliot, p. 200).

There is something of sublime reverence about this kind of graceful waiting. In the life of Christ and the example of the saints, we discern a quality of patience that is far more than a merely human strength of character: their patience is a fundamentally *theological* virtue, rooted in adoration and a loving self-transcendence towards God. This is where the Christian understanding of patience departs so markedly from, for example, the vision of the Stoics. Unlike the philosophers' somewhat grim and lonely model of individual self-mastery, Christians delight to discover patience within the rich intimacy of relationship with a gracious God of loving kindness.

Christian patience is at heart a practice of waiting on God. It is not primarily about waiting for some gratifying thing or outcome, but a commitment to waiting with and on and for the love of God. In his sensitive reflection on Mary's attentive posture in Fra Angelico's Annunciation fresco, Iain McGilchrist distinguishes this intensely relational demeanour of waiting on a person from the more self-referential stance of waiting for some impersonal object or event (McGilchrist, p. 152). The former is a patient, respectful nurturing of a desire that will, in good time, disclose itself. The latter is a grasping, utilitarian pursuit of a want, which is intolerant of diversion or delay.

The figure of Mary in the painting also portrays the fully *embodied* character of the virtue of patience. Mary waits with every muscle and every breath, her supreme bodily stillness reflecting an exquisite attentiveness of heart and soul to the divine summons. Contrast this sheer physical poise with the furrowed and fidgety impatience we experience in our minds and bodies whenever we resist and refuse the necessity of waiting.

It is salutary to realize how many kinds of waiting rage have become commonplace in our society. Shouting, swearing, gesturing, sometimes physically attacking, people react with their bodies to a perceived interruption on their precious time. From traffic jams to airport queues, from post office counters to retail checkouts, this phenomenon of physical and verbal aggression betrays the appalling potential for violence in people who have never learned the gentler embodiment of habitual patience.

A third characteristic of Christian patience is beautifully apparent in the Annunciation scene, as the angel and Mary wait each upon the other, in a posture of profoundly mutual respect. Here the artist beautifully captures the *social* dimension of patience in the enquiring gaze that neither hurries nor forces a response. Socially, theologically and bodily, the enactment of Christian patience is a matter of learning to bear with life, and one another, in graceful and whole-souled love.

The kindest virtue

The virtue of patience is about fostering a kindly relationship with our life in time. Instead of raging against the clock, patient souls learn to practise the skill underpinning all skills, which is to take the time to learn how to live and mature graciously as creatures of time.

I love the irony of this virtuous spiral. We can only learn patience by being patient about our practice of patience: and this is a cycle of moral and spiritual development that can take a whole lifetime! The poet Hermann Hesse describes this process beautifully:

> Patience is the most difficult thing of all and the only thing that is worth learning. All nature, all growth, all peace, everything that flowers and is beautiful in the world depends on patience, requires time, silence, trust, and faith in long-term processes which exceed any single lifetime, which are accessible to the insight of no one person, and which in their totality can be experienced only by peoples and epochs, not by individuals. (Hesse, p. 58)

Perhaps the full flowering of this lovely virtue can only be truly appreciated in the light of eternity. Certainly, there is a strong suggestion from psychological research that the people most capable of learning patience are those who are committed to some religious practice or spiritual transcendence (Schnitker and Emmons, pp. 177ff.). This is the approach that I shall cultivate throughout this book, offering a series of contemplative images and spiritual exercises designed to feed and encourage a faithful development of Christian patience.

God himself is the beginning and the end of all our human waiting. My prayer is that, together, we will learn the gifts of patience in a graceful and contemplative waiting on the God who waits for us.

Practicum – play the tune again

Patient practice in any sphere of life entails some form of repetition. From marathon running to mindfulness, we learn the necessary habits of mind and body by a repeated exercise of physical and spiritual muscles. Paradoxically, when it comes to learning patience, what we need to exercise is a kind of 'negative capability'[2] or a wise passivity akin to prayerful contemplation; but this, too, must be reinforced by repetition and intentional practice.

There are infinite ways to approach this form of practice. We might begin with a formal set-piece exercise that raises our awareness of the challenges of waiting, gradually working habits of attentive patience deep into the fabric of our souls. Repeating the exercise, with richer and fuller investment, like so many prayers gathered into a rosary, will intensify the commitment to holy patience within our time set aside from everyday busyness.

Sooner or later, however, we shall need to put our patience into practice within the hurly-burly of daily life. It will be the ordinary challenges of our mundane responsibilities and relationships, when we are less in control of the situation, that test the genuineness of our commitment to graceful waiting. And it will be the extraordinary times of shocking incapacity and fear that reveal the extent to which Christian patience has been moulded into our hearts.

One of my favourite poems by the Scottish writer Alastair Reid hints at the beautiful ways in which repetition and rehearsal leads naturally into reverence and holy waiting. In his 'Lesson in Music' (Reid, p. 88), he describes how the patient practice of a musical tune, over time, leads to deeper and deeper levels of artistic appreciation and self-discovery. At first there is an inevitably mechanical and self-conscious approach to the music. But, as the practitioner plays the tune over and again, we are drawn into a growing awareness of the contemplative flow between music and fingering, meaning and love, all as a wonderfully evocative 'arrangement of silence'.[3]

As a spiritual exercise to conclude this chapter, I invite you to read a poem or listen to a piece of music several times over. As you read or listen, slow down and try to practise an intentional 'negative capability' that makes space for the deeper levels of meaning to enfold you. Let yourself be surprised, moved, addressed and in some way transformed. Take some time in silence at the end of your exercise to gently absorb the lesson, and the rich gift, of graceful waiting.

Notes

1 Harned, *Patience*, p. 1, referring to *A New Dictionary of Christian Ethics*, 1986, and its forebear in 1967.

2 The phrase 'negative capability' was coined by John Keats, 'Letter to G. and T. Keats, 21 December 1817' in Rollins, p. 193.

3 A wonderful audio-recording by the poet is available on the Poetry Archive website. Available online, www.poetryarchive.org/poet /alastair-reid.

3

The Wilderness

Can God spread a table in the wilderness? (Psalm 78.19)

Steve has just lost his job. He knew that his career was going nowhere but, even so, it is terrifying to find himself in this strange no-man's land. The wilderness of waiting can be deeply unnerving. All his familiar securities have been swept away. His regular workmates, the shape of the week, his everyday routine, his salary payments, his identity, his confidence, are all dismantled. He is in an anxious wilderness now – learning to wait.

Joan has finished a long course of cancer treatment. She is tired and shockingly weak. She feels out of touch with the simple pleasures of ordinary life. Hardest of all, she doesn't know what lies ahead. Has the treatment worked? Or will she find out, like other people she knows, that her cancer has just been held in check? She waits for tests, waits for reassurance, waits for her confidence and energy to return, facing down the fears and uncertainties – feeling lost and alone in the wilderness of waiting.

Mary is in a miserable marriage. Phil is a vicar in a bruising multi-parish benefice. Gill's daughter is worryingly ill with anorexia. Bill is watching his beloved mother fall apart with dementia. Each one waits in their own wilderness – not knowing, not in control, powerless to move things along, unable to make everything all right again. This is the wasteland, the wilderness of waiting.

The wilderness is our first classroom in the school of patience. In this nowhere land, there is precious little for your comfort. This precarious place we now inhabit is like a bare desert, an unbounded expanse of sand and salt, where all the familiar scaffolding of life is blown away by the winds. It is scrubby, hostile territory, as wild within as without. This strange landscape is neither here nor there;

it's not the place we came from, nor the place we're going to. Lost space, lonely space, oh-so-liminal space.

> Wandering between two worlds, one dead,
> The other powerless to be born,
> With nowhere to rest my head,
> Like these, on earth I wait forlorn. (Matthew Arnold, 1855)

This is our wilderness experience of unfathomable waiting. Without signposts, we feel confused. Without shelter, we feel exposed. Without control, we feel horribly anxious. Yet strangely, this wilderness space can become a uniquely holy ground; through faith and hope and love and, above all, patience, the wilderness for Christians can become a place of glorious potential.

The archetypal desert

One of the great gifts of a religious tradition is to furnish our imagination with powerful stories. The image of the desert is one of the most evocative archetypes in our own Hebrew and Christian narrative, and it is an image that is also strikingly significant in many other religious traditions.

Again and again, we read of how God's people, through choice or necessity, are driven into the wilderness. The theme of the desert is central to much of the Old Testament, where it is often only in retrospect that God's people can look back on their wanderings as a honeymoon time for their relationship with God. As we read the unfolding narrative, we realize that this sacred wilderness has a special place in God's purposes, as a space of radical un-making and re-making, where the greatest saints learn the lessons of dangerous waiting on God.

The wilderness is a place of vision and commitment. Moses went into the wilderness to hear God's summons in the burning bush, and embrace his vocation to lead the people of Israel out of their slavery in Egypt. He gained the faith to guide them through a fearful wilderness, with countless testing experiences, towards God's Promised Land.

The wilderness is a place of sifting and refining. John the Baptist preached in the desert. Jesus was tempted in the desert. Paul, following his dramatic encounter with Christ, withdrew to the desert to pray and prepare for his apostolic ministry.

In the fiercest and most luminous ways, Christian ascetics view the desert as the ultimate school of the spirit. Metaphorically or literally, serious seekers after God find the necessary wilderness that will galvanize their quest. 'But the entrance fee to the desert comes perilously close to what I have struggled most of my life to avoid,' confessed one modern-day hermit: 'depression, chaos, loneliness, foolishness, weakness, insecurity, limitedness, helplessness, contingency, the terror of nothingness – all these are variations on the theme of void and death' (Jones, p. 55).

Stripped of the distractions that crowd our everyday life, the solitary soul comes face to face with the solitude of God. Generations of monks, hermits and mystics have sought this daring spaciousness in order to develop a truer perspective on life – wrestling and waiting on God alone.

Wilderness lessons

Such a sacred vision of the wilderness is in marked contrast to the mood of our age. I was reminded recently of the shallow restlessness of our times when scanning some holiday photos from Disneyworld. Every day members of the Disney team, dressed as Micky and Goofy, go out into the waiting lines for one purpose. Their task is to entertain and distract the customers who would otherwise find queueing intolerable. This is one of the many ways in which, younger and older, we collude with one another in a profound cultural rejection of the risks of wilderness waiting. In the desert, by contrast, we must inhabit a world devoid of shallow ornamentation or social 'staffing' where we abandon our comforting deceptions in order to engage a deeper and life-giving reality.

In this book, I aim to outline some of the practices that can bring such human, and spiritual, maturity to our necessary waiting. As we seek to understand, and to grow together in patience, I shall point out for each chapter two practices that we might adopt for daily life, together with one gift of grace, which is ours to embrace. Learning from the rich experience of the ascetic wilderness tradition, we shall explore the particular desert practices of surrender and struggle, and the surprising wilderness gift of sustenance.

The practice of surrender

Within the great sweep of the biblical narrative, we recognize that the wilderness is never the final symbol of the life of faith. It is a liminal space, a necessary interim, which becomes a sacred staging post along the road to a greater glory. The story neither begins nor ends here, but the waiting ground is essential to the transforming dynamic of grace, which will test and enlarge our souls, through all that the wilderness demands.

The famous anthropologist Arnold van Gennep (1960) introduced the idea of liminality as a key element in many social and religious rites of passage. At times of growth and development, or at points of transition between one stage of life and another, many societies find ways to ritualize the breaking down of old patterns in order to make way for something quite new. Like the breaking down of an outworn chrysalis, this pattern of separation from the old status, leading to a difficult and disorienting transitional phase that ushers in the possibility of a new maturity, has been replicated in all kinds of ancient and more modern experiences and rituals – from birth and puberty to the enactment of a wedding or an ordination. Part of the power of these ritual experiences lies in their recognition of the need for a positive spiritual engagement with the necessary 'molten' stage of liminality and deep transformation.

This positive and prayerful engagement is key to Jesus' relationship with the wilderness. Famously at the outset of his ministry he went into the wilderness for forty days to seek a radical new orientation for what lay ahead. We also read how, throughout his ministry, he continued to take periods of solitary prayer, early in the morning before his disciples had woken up, or late into the night in the agonizing hours of Gethsemane.

Away from the crowds and the clamour, Jesus learned to surrender to his true vocation. His desert experience was not just
some accident of history. The gospels suggest a whole-souled
intention and commitment on Jesus' part, which is underpinned
by the reassuring comment from the evangelist that it was God's
Spirit that directed him to go out into the wilderness (Luke 4.1).

The ascetic pattern of Jesus' obedience is one of willing surrender. He chooses to leave behind the 'normal' structures of time
and space, driven into the wilderness, and freely relinquishing
the need for certainty and control. In his protracted wilderness of
waiting, he learns to surrender fully to the word and will of God.

In contemporary language, we might speak of 'leaning in' to
the challenge of interim time where all that we once knew has
been wiped out, while what is still to come remains concealed. We
must surrender to the not-yet-knowing. In the deeply uncertain
and unsettling in-between time, we need the courage to admit the
passing of what is lost before we can be ready to greet the birth of
all that is too young to be born.

'What is being transfigured here is your mind,' writes the poet-
priest John O'Donohue, 'and it is difficult and slow to become
new.' Like Jesus, we are called to surrender faithfully to the sheer
vulnerability of the desert so that our hearts may be refined for
their 'arrival in the new dawn' (O'Donohue, pp. 119ff.).

We can trace the same pattern of single-minded surrender in
those thousands of serious believers, from the earliest centuries of
the church, who left the comforts of the city for a more authentic, less compromised form of Christian discipleship. First in the
Egyptian desert, then in the wilderness south of Palestine, then on
the steppes beyond Syria, the desert fathers and mothers embraced
the wilderness as a crucible for intense spiritual purification.

Wherever we find ourselves stripped down to the bare essen-
tials, we have entered into the wilderness, a place where we can
hear the whispers of God's voice in all their subtlety. Silent, solitary, seeking, surrendered, acutely receptive to the inviting word
of grace, we come to a desert of holy waiting on God.

It may not be easy to imagine our everyday frustrations and
delays as a kind of holy wilderness. Small roadblocks along the
way, or major tragedies that throw our whole lives into meltdown,

may not feel like an invitation to enter the sacred arena of God's wilderness. Yet the same practice of surrender is the key to an active encounter with the deeply liminal desert where God's grace waits to be discovered. We too must relinquish our need for certainty and control, and give up our comforting distractions and denials.

This is the *via negativa*, the radical letting-go of wilderness spirituality. Many of the saints and mystics have tried to describe this territory for us, and they can be our guides in the trackless wilderness of necessary waiting. Following Christ, they chose to step back into a desert of detachment and dispossession, determined to wait on God in a posture of radical contemplation.

One of the greatest misunderstandings of the spiritual life is the idea that a contemplative life is the heroic preserve of a few elite saints. In reality, this capacity for contemplative surrender to God's grace is not just a matter of private devotion, but a serious preparation for every practical aspect of our lives. Whether we are simply waiting for a parking place in the midst of a noisy city, or sitting in sacred vigil by the lonely bedside of a dying friend, it will be the practice of surrender that opens the door for God's Spirit to guide us into a 'new dawn'.

To surrender is essentially to admit that we are not ultimately in control of the time, or the final shape, of our lives. It is a practice very different from our habitual posturing, and often deceptive, self-assertion. It can feel very dry and desert-like, a path, as T. S. Eliot described in his *Four Quartets*, wherein there may be 'no ecstasy'. His searching poem, *East Coker*, harks back to the teaching of St John of the Cross to chart the necessary way of ignorance and dispossession, so searing that it can feel like 'the way in which you are not'. The profound paradox, which we can never know certainly except in hindsight, is that this dark and dangerous path becomes the road to our spiritual rebirth (Eliot, p. 201).

The grace of waiting begins with an act of spiritual surrender that is categorically different from hopelessness or simple despair. It is an act of faith in the promised future that God is graciously unfolding.

The Old Testament scholar Walter Brueggemann helpfully charted the shape of many scriptural narratives in terms of a

threefold movement from initial orientation, through uncomfortable dis-orientation, into an emerging glory of re-orientation
towards God's emerging new creation (Brueggemann, pp. 15ff.).
Our wilderness times can be seasons of profound and unwelcome
dis-orientation when we are reduced to a level zero of consoling
securities. Paradoxically, it is only when the deep discomfort of
the wilderness is honestly engaged, in a spirit of surrender that
countenances neither denial nor distraction, that we can hope to
discover God's vital presence. It is an essential interim time in
which our souls are being patiently transfigured for an unimagin-
ably greater glory.

The practice of struggle

Learning patience is often a fierce struggle. Anyone with an ounce
of spiritual sensitivity knows that there is nothing like the close
confinement of wilderness times to bring out our inner demons.

Perhaps this explains some of our extreme reluctance to accept,
let alone surrender to, necessary delay. What we experience in the
open tract of waiting, out beyond the pendulum edge of our habitual denials and busy distractions, is that our neurotic eruptions
find space to rise to the surface. Self-hatred, fear, anger, pride,
despair, pettiness, lust, bitterness, greed, cowardice, frustration
and sheer unmitigated rage can all burst into consciousness when
the ground is clear for thoughts that are normally suppressed
under the convenient mantle of 'business as usual'.

Take away the comfort blanket of control and we are propelled
into a howling psycho-spiritual desert. There, in the wilderness
of waiting, we will be confronted with the inflated power of negative thoughts – our own most familiar demons – taunting and
tempting us with a destructive power that can wreak havoc in our
anxious souls.

This is how it was for Jesus. The temptations were shockingly
real and terribly personal. His venture into the wilderness is graphically described in the gospels as a period of profound struggle.
The ferociousness of this time is hard to overestimate. The evangelists speak of 'wild beasts' circling around him (Mark 1.13).

Artists depict dark demons with lurid shadows, posing around him and poisoning the air. Writers in the classic spiritual tradition invoke a whole menagerie of demonic figures to convey the intensity of the struggle that Jesus engaged during those bitter days in his spiritual wilderness.

Most of us, naturally enough, prefer to avoid the struggle. We would rather hide behind our shallow distractions than face the dreadful inner challenges of waiting – where we meet our fears face to face – fears of powerlessness, of insignificance, or loneliness, of sheer and utter dependence on God.

The remarkable example of Jesus, like that of many saints and ascetics, lies in his voluntary engagement with this struggle, with a commitment to deepen and purify his obedience to the Father. It is worth pondering this radical determination when we face our own wilderness periods. For Jesus, the period of waiting was never a purely passive interim that had to be meekly endured. Whether in the wilderness beyond the Jordan, or in the dark night of Gethsemane where he awaited a cruel death, we find Jesus very actively engaged in hand-to-hand wrestling with the demons that would obstruct God's gracious purposes.

This is a truly active mode of waiting which we need to rediscover and practise in our impatient generation. We would rather fritter away our days in mindless distraction than get down to the hard spiritual business of grappling our inner demons. It is so easy to anaesthetize our fears through addictive eating, drinking or social media. Jesus never wasted these wild struggles. He followed the call into the desert, as many saints before and after him have testified, precisely in order to face its wild struggles on the frontline of spiritual combat.

The actualities of warfare are terribly familiar to people who have held military command. Veteran commanders know that different contexts and theatres of engagement generate quite distinctive types of conflict. The challenges of desert warfare, for example, will be quite different from the challenges of jungle warfare.

Experienced spiritual directors observe that, in the battle for the human spirit, there are similar subtleties to negotiate. The busy confusions of life in our everyday world are like a tangled jungle for the spirit, where we are often blind to the enemy of human nature who subverts and undermines our spiritual well-being through the very hiddenness of his distractions. Wilderness times are different. In stark contrast to the spiritual guerrilla warfare of everyday busyness, the struggles of the desert are more black and white. The enemy of human nature is horribly and unquestionably active on the stage; and the temptations of the desert, although fearful, may be much more readily identified. For those who have the courage to engage in this territory, although the battle may be fierce, it is the sheer overtness of spiritual conflict that makes determined progress towards greater maturity a relatively straightforward affair.

Learning from Jesus, then, there are two aspects of his spiritual struggle that can strengthen us for our own times of wilderness waiting. The first great strength that Jesus embodies is the wisdom to name temptations for what they are. In his long, hard days and nights in the desert, Jesus faced repeated temptations to shortcut his path to glory. It can be the same for any of us in the depths of waiting, when we chase after any easy solution that will cut short the anxieties and uncertainties of our present wilderness. The enemy can be very plausible, and it is not easy to stay present to the deeper challenges of the struggle, rather than rushing forward in impatience and fear. Recognizing the true seriousness of our struggle is the first step to greater spiritual maturity.

The second strength that Jesus exemplifies in the wilderness is the calm assertiveness with which he resists the enemy. Easy escapes are put down with a firm and patient resolve; and noisy demons silenced by the word of God. Such steadiness under fire does not come lightly, and I would not suggest that any of us find the temptations of the wilderness particularly easy to brush off. Demons of simmering resentment, or lurking despair, or cruel impatience, or foolish haste will circle around us again and again. We will need to learn, together with Jesus, first to recognize and then to resist the unnerving and vicious darkness that comes from our spiritual enemy.

All this is tough spiritual practice. We are not born with moral courage; and no one, including Jesus, finds it easy to practise patience in the trackless wilderness of waiting. Whether we enter this wilderness through choice, or we are confronted with necessary waiting against our will, then we will have much to learn from Jesus about the ascetic practice of surrender and struggle that will guide us forward in grace.

The profound archetypal image of the wilderness helps us to understand our necessary waiting, not merely as a minor irritant on the smooth surface of life, but as a deeper tectonic shift in the spiritual foundations of our whole being. Choosing to stay with the struggle, not ducking out through distraction, will be the route to a new level of wisdom and maturity. The Spirit who called Jesus into the wilderness is the same Spirit who will strengthen us in our own struggles, so that, as the early followers of Christ testified, when we resist the devil he will surely flee (James 4.7). This will be the practice, and the proof, of authentic Christian patience and staying power.

The gift of sustenance

In each chapter, as we explore the rich images of waiting with Christ, I hope to indicate that there is always a gift to discover. The grace of waiting is not all grim determination, but a surprising discovery – even in the midst of deep and ongoing uncertainty – of the beautiful gifts that God promises to those who wait faithfully on his promises. In the wilderness, we will be graced with the gift of sustenance.

Looking back on the rich narratives of faith, one of the most epic stories of wilderness waiting must be the long forty years through which the children of Israel wandered in the desert of Sinai. It is one of those stories that has been told and retold within the Judeo-Christian family, a foundational experience in the unfolding saga of how God's people came to fully grasp their identity and unique spiritual vocation.

The children of Israel were on their way to the Promised Land. But such is the convoluted nature of individual human and social experience that their journey could not follow the direct route. There could be no quick and straightforward transition from the house of slavery to the land flowing with milk and honey. Instead, they faced a protracted period of testing and waiting, a pilgrim detour on a massive scale.

The story of the Exodus paints a wonderful phenomenological picture of wilderness faith. The Israelite's hazardous journey, fraught with hardships and uncertainties on every page, reflects the deep story of every pilgrim soul. In this pilgrimage of liminality, the wilderness itself becomes a major motif, from the first solitary encounter where Moses meets the living God in the burning bush of Horeb (Exodus 3.2–6). The desert is a fitting backdrop for a revelation that gradually takes the people from idolatry towards pure and faithful worship. It is a landscape so utterly devoid of form and familiarity that its very barrenness matches, by way of contrast, the overwhelming glory of a transcendent God.

Paradox and awe continue throughout the unfolding Exodus narrative. Moses returns from Mount Horeb to confront Pharaoh on behalf of the enslaved Israelites, with the specific demand to 'let my people go, so that they may celebrate a festival to me in the wilderness' (Exodus 5.1). Against the proud wealth of Egypt, the desert symbolizes a relinquishment of human preoccupations, so that God alone should become Israel's sole concern. This is the heart of spiritual worship, to forgo the familiarity of everyday human idolatries, in single-minded response to the call of a living God.

The outworking of this call leads across the Red Sea and into a precarious wilderness where the Israelites must have imagined that they would surely die (Exodus 14.11; Numbers 21.5). Fearful and fractious, they grumble and complain about Moses and his leadership, and the God who has brought them from Egypt to such a 'wretched place' (Numbers 20.5).

Here is the beautiful paradox of the wilderness, to the eyes of faith. In the midst of all the anxiety and deprivation, God is close at hand, protecting and guiding, reassuring and providing through a generous providence of miraculous food and drink. We read of quails and manna falling from the heavens, of water streaming from the rock. We sense the puzzlement of people trying to make sense of these strange phenomena: the word 'manna' means 'what is it?' We smile at those who tried to temper their trust in divine providence with a touch of human prudence by stockpiling more manna than was needed for their daily bread. They learned their lesson when the larder stocks turned rotten on the morrow (Exodus 16.16–21).

It is an epic story of gratuitous provision, and a kind of sustenance that resonates with cosmic and theological symbolism. The true and living God is leading his people, not merely from the physical slavery of Egypt, but from their spiritual enslavement to a false and greedy idolatry, and from their anxious captivity to human calculations to a radical dependence on the sheer grace and glory of God.

This far-reaching shift of spiritual sensibilities is embodied in the shift of their physical appetites – from the sensuously recalled 'fleshpots' of Egypt (Exodus 16.3) to the living bread, the manna that comes down from heaven. This is the free gift of sustenance for those who are prepared to wait in faith on the goodness of the living God.

Our wilderness of waiting is a school of humility where God leads us, not to destroy us, but to teach the lessons that only delayed gratification can impart – 'by letting you hunger, then by feeding you with manna . . . in order to make you understand that one does not live by bread alone' (Deuteronomy 8.3).

For those who believe and put their trust in God, even the wilderness of waiting becomes a place of unlikely hospitality and grace. Sustenance, at every turn, is given to them. Prophets are fed by ravens (1 Kings 17.6). The Son of God is attended by angels (Matthew 4.11). The grace of patient waiting is rewarded in gifts of beauty and abundance. Looking back on the lessons of the wilderness, a later generation of prophetic souls could rejoice in the overwhelming blessing that the desert years had come to represent for God's people.

> The wilderness and the dry land shall be glad,
> the desert shall rejoice and blossom;
> like the crocus it shall blossom abundantly,
> and rejoice with joy and singing.
> The glory of Lebanon shall be given to it,
> the majesty of Carmel and Sharon.
> They shall see the glory of the LORD,

the majesty of our God.
Strengthen the weak hands,
and make firm the feeble knees . . .

For waters shall break forth in the wilderness,
and streams in the desert . . .

They shall obtain joy and gladness,
and sorrow and sighing shall flee away. (Isaiah 35.1–3, 6, 10)

Practicum – a wilderness walkabout

Learning patience is always a matter of concrete practice more
than abstract theory. The exercises in this book aim to instil some
of the bodily and spiritual habits that will patiently build our
capacity for graceful waiting. I hope that you will make time to
experiment with some of these suggestions, and perhaps to incor-
porate them into your regular pattern of spiritual reflection.

To explore more deeply the material in this chapter, I invite you
to plan a walk into some kind of 'wild space', which is to a certain
extent beyond your comfort zone. It may be a depopulated area
on the edge of a city, or a tract of countryside that is off the beaten
track. Let your choice of a physically liminal landscape resonate
with your spiritual intention to attend to your inner dynamics of
wilderness waiting.

The practice of walking as a spiritual exercise has very ancient
roots. It is an excellent way of calming the mind, allowing deep-
felt issues to come quietly to the surface for our attention. Try to
plan the walk so that you can give unhurried time and be attentive
to the whole experience of encountering this 'wilderness'. As you
walk, I invite you to notice some of the past and present issues of
necessary waiting that may present a challenge for you, and to
experiment that the practices of surrender and struggle.

Notice what happens as you enter the rhythm of walking and
explore the sense of movement through time and space. What does
it feel like to move through the 'wild spaces' of your inner and
outer landscape? What does it take to surrender to the experience

of liminality as an important part of your own spiritual journey? As your walk progresses, try to engage with determination and faith any struggles that arise, especially those that help you to be deeply honest about the bleaker parts of your experience.

If you make your walking expedition into a spiritual exercise, then you can expect that God will provide for you in gracious and unexpected ways along the way. Keep your eyes and ears open, and make space in your heart for a quiet expectancy. You may be surprised by something unexpectedly lovely, or be greeted by a warm and friendly face; or, perhaps, some deeper sustenance may come through an inner recognition of how God is at work to stretch and mature you. Accept gratefully whatever blessing comes – by way of encouragement or fresh hope – as God's generous provision for your pilgrimage of faith.

Your physical exposure to an unfamiliar or unbounded landscape will mirror some significant spiritual encounters, from the past or the present, with the 'wild spaces' of waiting. Notice your fears. Name your temptations. By surrendering to the experience, and engaging any accompanying inner struggle, you will exercise some of those vital spiritual muscles that will patiently build your capacity for waiting on God.

When you return home, you may want to speak with someone about your experience and reflections on this exercise. Or it may be helpful to write some notes and reflections in a journal. To consolidate your practical exercise, find a time to re-read one of the biblical narratives of the wilderness, such as Psalm 78.

4

The Wine Press

Why are your robes red, and your garments like theirs who tread the wine press? (Isaiah 63.2)

Nick and Debbie are young parents. When I search them out in the Neonatal Intensive Care Unit, they are pacing up and down in the waiting area. Nick is on the phone to a friend. He is talking angrily about mistakes and mismanagement. Debbie is toying with a drink, trying to keep awake after a long night worrying about their critically ill child. Baby Oscar, two days old and dangerously premature, is in theatre for major abdominal surgery. His waiting parents have asked to see the chaplain.

I am not sure who coined the phrase, 'the wine press of waiting', but I learned it from fellow-chaplains who share the weary road of fretful waiting as a regular part of hospital ministry. It perfectly describes the long haul of care and worry borne by parents and others who have responsibility for people with major health problems and disabilities.

Treading the wine press is the archetype of arduous and unremitting labour. In traditional viticulture, it is the task of a barefoot peasant, a bonded serf, who is put to work tramping the ripened fruit in a waist-high vat, until the wine press runs with gallons of blood-red grape juice. It is a powerful image, which often comes to mind when I speak with people who feel crushed and exhausted by a labour of waiting that has no end in sight.

For Nick and Debbie, their ordeal in the wine press is just beginning. Like many people, they will have to adapt to years of anxiety, adjustment and additional care, as the full impact of Oscar's complex medical condition becomes apparent. I can only pray that they will grow in strength and patience for the days ahead, and find support along the way.

The mystic wine press

In the medieval church, the wine press was a common metaphor for the suffering work of Christ. The mystic wine press was a favourite image on church walls and altarpieces, in books, woodcuts and stained-glass windows. We can imagine the instinctive kinship felt in the wine-growing communities of central Europe for this graphic figure of Christ, tramping out the harvest so that life-giving wine might flow in abundance.

Emphases vary, Christ being portrayed sometimes as the one treading the grapes, sometimes as the trodden. Biblical images merge freely in a richly symbolic tradition that dates back to the patristic era, when Gregory the Great brought the two ideas into a fusion. 'He has trodden the winepress alone in which he was himself pressed, for with his own strength he patiently overcame suffering' (Schiller, p. 228).

Artists portray Christ standing erect and strong, pinned to the waist-high beam, his limbs constrained within the vat, pounding out the rich wine that flows beneath his feet. Some picture him as the Man of Sorrows, pressed down beneath the beam, his back bent under the weight of the screw mechanism that squeezes out the precious juices. Often his clothes are blood-red. Sometimes he seems to have fallen into the vat, as if to identify his own body with the clusters of fruit being trampled.

Many paintings highlight eucharistic motifs. The precious juice flows into a communion chalice. Sometimes a parallel apparatus mills the grain to produce a sacred host. More explicit meditations show the blood of Christ exuding under the weight of the wine press, whose screw is slowly turned by pious angels. Meanwhile, the precious flow of mingled blood and juice is collected by a company of saints, who wait to taste the first fruits of their redemption. Alongside this potent visual imagery, we read various interpretive texts from scripture: 'I have trodden the wine press alone' (Isaiah

63.3); 'For the sake of the joy that was set before him he endured the cross, disregarding its shame' (Hebrews 12.2); 'Surely he has borne our infirmities and carried our diseases' (Isaiah 53.4).

These artists and mystical theologians of the Middle Ages inhabited a different thought-world from our own, but their iconography tapped into a rich vein of understanding of the work of Christ. They intuited how the toilsome processes of wine-making provided a powerful analogy for the patient and costly work of soul-making. It takes time, and patient labour, to work from the first harvest of fresh fruit to the final yield of clear, new wine. And at the heart of this long labour of love stands the wine press of affliction.

Under pressure

How do we begin to address the problem of extended suffering? There are no simplistic answers, and the wisest theologians and pastors hold back from pretending any easy solutions for people whose entire lives are shaped by caring and pain. Looking back to the New Testament, we find a particularly evocative word in St Paul's writings about Christian suffering. He uses the word 'affliction' (*thlipsis* in Greek) to write about the experience of living under pressure, sometimes for unbearably long periods of time. The word carries echoes of slavery and duress, and is shot through with theological memories of the afflictions of God's people under Egyptian taskmasters, and the long years of oppression and exile.

The noun *thlipsis* comes from a verb that means literally 'to press', 'to squash' or 'to hem in'. In his epistles, St Paul writes of this 'affliction' as a particular burden of saints and apostles who are called, in one way or another, to bear pressure and tribulation as part of the continuing suffering of Christ for the redemption of the world.

These 'afflictions' are a recurring theme in the Corinthian letters where St Paul, writing from his own experience, develops a profoundly paradoxical theology of consolation through suffering, which seems to anticipate our later medieval imagery of the mystic wine press (2 Corinthians 1.3–9; 4.16–18; 6.4ff.; 7.2–4; 8.1–2). He describes the mounting pressure of affliction (*thlipsis*), which is felt as Christians take their part in those trials and tribulations, learning to bear them, and to share them, in intimate union with Christ himself. Enfolded within this solidarity of love comes a profound consolation (*parakleseos*), as the believer is yoked together with Christ in his suffering and passion. Out of the fullness (*pleroma*) of Christ, this pressure (*thlipsis*) creates a bountiful overflow of grace, a super-abundance of consolation and blessing.

This extended metaphor that St Paul develops has been explained by Anthony Harvey in terms of the hydrostatic principle, which is famously associated with Archimedes in his bathtub. Imagine a bowl or a tub that is partly full of water: with further topping up, it may simply be filled to its own capacity. But when the vessel is filled beyond its capacity, then it begins to spill over in a generous surplus which can water the ground all about, or even be collected by others. This is the dynamic in the Corinthian letters, as the pressure of affliction displaces showers of grace, like water. 'Christ's sufferings are awarded in such abundance that they *overflow* into the life of Paul, as a result of which the encouragement which derives from it *overflows* beyond Paul's capacity to contain it and yields blessing to others' (Harvey, p. 121).

This dynamic of overflowing abundance imbues St Paul's theology of affliction with a very different meaning from the trials borne by, for example, his proud Stoic contemporaries. Christians bear their trials as a participation in the fullness and generosity of Christ. So, St Paul does not boast of terrible hardships as evidence of his own endurance, or as a sign of indifference to mental or physical pain. Rather, his emphasis is always on his inherent weakness, through which he is enabled to boast of the strength of the risen Christ. It is in solidarity with Christ, eternally crucified and risen, that St Paul learns the deepest paradox of his own very human experience: that, while death may be at work in his own afflictions, yet consolation and new life are released to overflow for the sake of others (2 Corinthians 4.12).

The practice of steadfastness

What does all this mean in practice; and what might we usefully learn for ourselves and for others called into the winepress of waiting?

The theological imagery that unites our afflictions to those of Christ gives us a clue to our own deep practice of patience. Christian patience is modelled on, and borne in solidarity with, the suffering love and risen grace of Christ. The image of Christ, actively and willingly treading the wine press is the paradigm for our own steadfastness, patient endurance and hope. Learning patience will require this same commitment from ourselves, actively and willingly, to practise steadfastness under affliction, in order to resist evil and to grow in grace.

Heidi and Dan were parents whom I came to know when they were awaiting the birth of their first son, Joshua. Prenatal tests had predicted a high risk that their baby could have spina bifida; and a series of ultrasound scans suggested such a degree of deformity that they were strongly advised to consider termination. Heidi and Dan were a professional couple, experienced and intelligent people, who shared a deep Christian faith. They agonized over the options given to them, wanting neither to harden their hearts so as to casually terminate a long-awaited pregnancy, nor to underestimate the enormous challenges that would confront them if Joshua was born with major disabilities. After much prayer, and upheld by the loving and non-judgemental compassion of family and friends, they decided to go ahead with the pregnancy.

Six years on they are proud parents of a happy, intelligent, but moderately disabled child who will always need extra care and understanding. They have borne all the normal heartaches of parenthood and more, learning year by year how to sustain that delicate balance between patience and assertiveness, gracefulness and grit, which all parents of disabled children need if they are to navigate the challenges of social, educational and health care systems. They have supported Joshua through a multitude of hospital procedures, battled to gain access to appropriate schooling, challenged prejudicial and defeatist attitudes from unthinking neighbours and professionals, and worked with all their powers to negotiate the best possible social support that will allow their son to integrate and flourish alongside other children.

Dan and Heidi do not regard themselves as heroic or special, and they refrain from judging families who have made a different choice in respect of a potentially disabled child. What is remarkable about them is the quality of patience that they have learned in the midst of their afflictions, and the degree of steadfastness with which they tackle the challenges of a family life that is never going to be plain sailing.

Their kind of patience is not resignation. It is different from passivity or inaction in the face of tribulation. This active and committed character of Christian steadfastness distinguishes authentic patience from a more supine and fatalistic approach, which can be a parody of submission to the supposed 'will of God'. Heidi and Dan have never capitulated to the forces that would disadvantage their son or diminish their own humanity. Instead they have developed the kind of spiritual muscle that can sustain them in patience and perseverance for the long haul, and even bring joy and sparkle into the lives of others. In the heavy wine press of constant caring, they have learned a more athletic patience which 'is the emergence of freedom within the domain where necessity reigns' (Harned, p. 107).

The patient practice of steadfastness under affliction is sadly counter-cultural. In our age of instant gratification, it is rare to find people who will embrace long-term challenges without whingeing and self-pity. In the case of Heidi and Dan, the grace and patience with which they bear the burdens of daily care for Joshua reflects a great deal of their immense humanity and mature faith.

In my own experience, I have tried to engage something of a similarly active patience through the practice of long-distance pilgrimage walking. Taking time out each year to walk several hundred kilometres on the Camino de Santiago has become a very physical and embodied practice of spiritual steadfastness – what I playfully describe as my 'retreat on legs'. Pressing on, mile after mile, through rugged mountains and lush valleys, deep forests and dry desert plateaus, becomes a powerfully active metaphor for the whole life of faith. I often use these times to engage in serious and sympathetic intercession for those whose lives are a constant wine press of strenuous caring.

There are lessons that can only be embraced in the midst of the journey. Patience is learned and practised in the details. What it means to cope with our own mental weariness and irritability, while reckoning with aching limbs and cruel blisters, can be a salutary lesson in the steadfastness that many patient souls develop through their own tribulations and the labour of love and care for family members.

I remember a particularly gruelling section of the pilgrimage route which ran through an ancient limestone region of France. Weeks of dry heat had created a thick layer of chalky dust along the trail, which turned to something like quick-setting concrete with the first drops of morning rain. Walking through this terrain was the most exhausting and frustrating experience, as heavy lumps of chalk mud weighed down our boots. We had to practise endless patience to scrape and gouge out the clinging mud before it set solid under our feet, stopping and starting every few hundred meters to shift the accumulated load.

Walking a pilgrimage trail is both a choice and a discipline, which brings us into fellowship with countless faithful saints and pilgrims who have walked the Christian path ahead of us. Together we walk the mile, and share the journey, learning afresh the age-old lessons of patience and steadfastness, and tasting the rich joys of companionship, which bind us closer to Christ and to one another.

The practice of solidarity

The cathedral of Notre Dame at Le Puy en Velay in the Auvergne is a famous historic gathering point for pilgrims. Waiting there to commence a long and rigorous stretch out into the surrounding hill country, I gazed at a semi-relief sculpture high on the western wall. It shows a small company of pilgrims, men and women, old and young, leaning on each other's arms and shoulders for support. Like many of the medieval pilgrims who once passed through the cathedral, several of the figures were sick or lame or blind. Stepping out together, despite their individual infirmities, they found the strength to go forward on the pilgrim route in search of healing.

I often recall these weary pilgrims when, in my work at the hospital, I come alongside people undergoing particularly strenuous therapies. Our haematology ward specializes in stem cell transplants entailing very high-dose chemotherapy treatment for people with blood cancers. Often patients have to stay in hospital for weeks on end, kept in isolated rooms to protect them from infection, while they undergo the enormously toxic treatment that carries high risks of side effects and, in some cases, of death.

My role is to offer kindness and encouragement and, for those who seek spiritual support, to assure them of prayer. Sharing the load with these patients and their families is an object lesson in steadfastness and solidarity, while they have no choice but to embrace the sufferings on the path ahead, and to wait for the uncertain outcome of a highly challenging treatment regime.

Christian solidarity is, on one level, a devastatingly simple practice. According to St Paul's maxim we are urged to 'bear one another's burdens, and in this way [to] fulfil the law of Christ' (Galatians 6.2). Jesus' teaching puts it more graphically. He paints the picture of shouldering and sharing his yoke, so as to learn from his gentleness and humility (Matthew 11.29). It is an apt image of patience under pressure, reflecting the way that untrained oxen would be teamed up with an older partner who would school them in the disciplines of the plough.

Later in the gospel narrative we read about Simon of Cyrene, drafted in to help carry Jesus' cross on the road to Calvary (Matthew 27.32). Roman soldiers, apparently, had a legal right to 'impress' any provincial to carry their heavy gear. It seems that Simon had little choice in the matter: yet, his preparedness to walk the grim road, and carry the burden of a condemned man, has endured as a potent symbol of Christian solidarity under suffering and oppression.

Patients often tell me that they have little choice in the matter of their suffering. And yet, there can be something redemptive in the way that people choose to give help to one another along the road. I am often impressed by the willingness with which people with cancer will undertake experimental treatments with high

risks of side effects, not so much for the sake of an unlikely benefit to themselves, but because of their commitment to improving
treatment options for those who will be in the same difficult posi-
tion at some point in the future.

The empathy and the willingness to draw alongside another
person in their suffering is a wonderful expression of human solidarity. At a deeper level, it also reflects the truth of God's intimate involvement in our human afflictions, which was embodied
to the uttermost in the sufferings of Christ, and in the consolation
(*paraklēseos*) that still sustains us through the ongoing ministry of
the Holy Spirit, the Comforter (*paraklēton*) (John 14.16).

One very practical expression of Christian solidarity is the practice of patient intercessory prayer. Unlike the Stoics, who taught
that those who stand most firmly are those who stand alone,
Christians believe that we are strongest when we stand united in
Christ, and sharing with one another in the fellowship of his sufferings (Philippians 3.10). Our commitment to pray with and for others is, in itself, an expression of loving solidarity in the wine press
of waiting: because prayer is an act of steadfast waiting on God.

Whether we pray for ourselves or intercede for our fellow-
pilgrims in their sufferings, the intention we offer creates a space
where it becomes possible to wait for the stirrings of God. This
is the work of active intercession, generous and holy waiting in
communion with Christ, where, in the grace of his Spirit, we can
pray for the power to be gentle, the strength to be humble and the
patience to show compassion to all who need our care.

The gift of simplicity

'What might be the gift in this?' It is a rather daring question, but
one that, as a chaplain, I have sometimes put to people who face
enormous challenges in life. Surprisingly often, people respond pos-
itively. Even in the cruel wine press, where it seems we have so little
choice and freedom of manoeuvre, there is a grace to receive which
we may not discover under any other circumstances. For many
people, this gift is the grace of a sweet and liberating simplicity.

''Tis the gift to be simple,' according to the old Shaker lyric. Joseph Brackett's gentle song trips along with the lightness and *joie de vivre* of a dance tune, unencumbered by weight and worry.

Simplicity is a necessity for the long-haul pilgrim; and it becomes the cheerful gift of the seasoned pilgrim who has learned to travel light. Those who have learned to shed their excess baggage, and strip down their inflated expectations of life, are the ones who are ready to bow and to bend, and not be ashamed.

There is a virtue of simplicity in a child, who has not yet reckoned with the heaviness and complexities of self-important adulthood. But far more beautiful is the serene simplicity of the elder, the one bruised and battered by experience, who has worked through to life's essential treasures of humility, patience and compassion.

In the wine press of suffering, the gift of simplicity emerges as a beautiful alternative to bitterness. I see this simplicity on the faces of parents who rejoice when their disabled child is able to take part in 'normal' pleasures. I recognize it in the room of dying patients who gaze contentedly at the garden, the skies and the birds through their window. I watch a growing simplicity in the attitude of pilgrims who have walked through their impatience and desire for control to find a more liberated appreciation of the hospitality and gifts of an unpredictable journey.

As the German theologian Meister Eckhart observed, great human souls grow 'by subtraction'. This is the real but costly gift of the wine press, where everything that is not pure and life-giving must be crushed and destroyed in order to release the sweet juices that will ferment into a rich wine.

Practicum – contemplative baking

I have kept in mind throughout this chapter the spiritual challenge facing people who are tasked with a lifetime of waiting on others. What does graceful waiting mean in the seemingly endless wine press of dependence, anxiety and sheer hard work? It may be appropriate, therefore, as a spiritual exercise at the end of this chapter, to explore the possibilities for patience in the practice of everyday domestic hospitality and care.

A friend of mine who is a nutritionist introduced me to the idea of 'mindful' or 'contemplative' baking. So often we approach the necessities of domestic life with impatient attitudes of resentment, irritability and haste, losing sight of the intrinsic beauty of the task before us. Home baking is one such task – basic, elemental, loving and sustaining – and it is a task that cannot be rushed.

As you think through the implications of this chapter for your own life, see if you can find a time when you can practise patience in your home kitchen, by preparing good food for your family, for a guest, or simply for yourself. The ideal exercise for this purpose is the extended task of baking bread; but if this is not a realistic option for you, then feel free to adapt the exercise to some other home-made specialty.

First, you will need to focus on gathering your *ingredients*. To make bread, you require the simplest staples of flour, yeast, salt and water: but what a story lies behind each of those elements! As you assemble these basics of life, let your mind and your body connect in solidarity with all those whose labour has brought them to your kitchen. Feel the softness of the flour, and remember the process of milling which slowly grinds the tough kernel of wheat to release the powdered silk that can feed us. Let your imagination range over the long labour of farming: the ploughing and sowing, the harvesting and threshing, the milling and sifting, the packaging and distribution. As you finger the flour, feel the sun and the earth, the wind and the rain, which have blessed this crop for your kitchen – and give thanks.

Take your time to appreciate the other ingredients as you assemble them. Notice your own contribution as you reflect in solidarity on the labours of others. Did you go out to buy fresh yeast for this batch of baking? Yeast is a living organism, which others have farmed in commercial vats and prepared for sale. Who paid the bills for the plentiful supply of clean, fresh water that we take so readily for granted? Long miles of pipeline connect your kitchen to the reservoirs that collect the gift of rain, to be purified and pumped out to millions of households and industries across the land. As for the salt, one spoonful represents a tiny expenditure in monetary terms; but as you reflect on the deep back story of mining and processing that goes into each grain, you may sense some parallels with the financially undervalued labours of love that have brought you to this point of caring.

Giving time to appreciate each simple ingredient connects us with the steadfastness and solidarity of countless neighbours, near and far.

The second step is the *mixing* and *kneading*. Putting our own physical effort into baking, with or without the help of electrical appliances, can be a surprisingly spiritual experience. My clenched knuckles that pound the dough may transmit anger as well as determination, frustration as well as hope. Yet through the vigour of my manual working and stretching, and the secret alchemy of biological processes at work within the dough, something transformative starts to take place, as a whole new biochemical nature begins to arise. Perhaps something cathartic might also be released in my soul?

The joy and challenge of baking bread is that it entails a necessary *waiting* stage. After the energy and activity of mixing and kneading, we move into passive mode. The dough must rise without further effort on our part. Silent processes of fermentation deep within the lump of dough are working to release the thousands of micro-bubbles that will cause the bread to rise.

Interestingly, the baker's word for this waiting stage is 'proving'. The verb is used in a similar way in other traditional contexts when farmers speak of the 'proving' of livestock, or the 'proving' of crops to describe the time it takes for their full strength and vitality to emerge. While the dough is 'proving' we have to wait and see: will the quality of the yeast and the vigour of our kneading 'prove' sufficient for a good bloom to emerge? There is an element of unpredictability; and our patience and trust will be put to the test as we wait through one, or often two, periods of proving before the loaf is ready to go into the oven.

The essential hiddenness of this stage is full of spiritual significance. It is not surprising that Jesus offered the unseen, organic work of fermenting yeast as a micro-parable of the kingdom (Matthew 13.33). The woman in his story was baking a very large batch of bread, using three measures – or about sixty pounds – of flour; so we might imagine she was preparing for a very special and generous occasion. Despite her best preparations, she is now at the mercy of forces beyond her control that will make or mar the hoped-for celebration.

Bill Vanstone's reflection on waiting captures very beautifully the hidden tensions of this time. For the one who waits 'the world discloses itself in its heights and in its depths, as wonder and terror, as blessing and threat. Man [*sic*] becomes, so to speak, the sharer with God of a secret – the secret of the world's power of meaning' (Vanstone, p. 112).

The secret will be revealed and celebrated only after the final stage of *baking* in the oven – another period of waiting during which, perhaps, you might be attending to many other necessary acts of care and hospitality – washing up, clearing tables, preparing a meal. This is the time to reflect on all that has gone into such a simple act of domestic kindness, and to give thanks for what has been 'proved' emotionally and spiritually in the process.

However you may have performed this exercise, whether in the extended practice of baking a batch of fresh bread, or through some shorter exercise of real or imagined kitchen work, I hope that our contemplative exploration of the meaning of waiting may illuminate some of the latent sacramentality within all of our work and care and hospitality.

As you give thanks, and share the bread that you have baked, take time to honour the patience that it represents in this simple prayer of appreciation.

Be gentle when you touch bread.
Let it not lie uncared for, unwanted.
So often bread is taken for granted.
There is such beauty in bread;
beauty of sun and soil,
beauty of patient toil.
Wind and sun have caressed it.
Christ often blessed it.
Be gentle when you touch bread.
(Anonymous)

5

The Watch

Stay here and keep watch with me. (Matthew 26.38, NIV)

On the Mount of Olives there is a small sculpture carved into the stone wall of a church. It shows Christ in Gethsemane crouching over the rock of agony. His body weighs heavily onto the ground, while both hands grip the rock that upholds his weary head.

The story of the Agony in the Garden is a profound study in divine-human waiting. It seems curious that the gospel writers describe more detail of Jesus' anguish in Gethsemane than they disclose of the cross itself. Many theologians make the point that the depth of Christ's passion is found here. It is in the terrible prayers of Gethsemane that we see Jesus waiting on the Father, wrestling to relinquish control over his fate. While the ordeal of crucifixion must have caused the greater physical pain, the evangelists suggest that Jesus' piercing spiritual agony came during those dark hours in the garden when 'his sweat became like great drops of blood falling down on the ground' (Luke 22.44).

This rings true to our own experience: the worst of times is the waiting time. So often it is the anticipation of suffering that causes the greatest agony. When someone is waiting for a biopsy result, they imagine the worst. When a serious diagnosis is confirmed, they rehearse in their minds every kind of terrifying treatment and dreadful outcome. It is the same when we are waiting to tackle an angry colleague, or face a hostile neighbour. The anticipation of coming conflict can bring far more grief and heartache than the actual showdown that follows.

Prostrate in the Garden, stretched between hope and unimaginable dread, we see in Jesus what it means to watch and pray. 'If it is possible', he prays that the cup of pain will pass from him.

But if not, 'if this cannot pass unless I drink it, your will be done' (Matthew 26.39–42). Clinging on to the rock of agony, Jesus embraces the full truth of his powerlessness to control the coming course of events. In an astonishing act of relinquishment, before he is finally handed over to those who will brutalize and kill him, he freely hands himself over to the providential grace of his Father. Before being bound by those who will drag him off to his enemies, he begs his friends to stay with him, to watch and to pray.

In this chapter, we shall reflect on what such 'watching' must entail.

The slow watches of the night

Ancient societies knew the vital importance of watching. Without benefit of electric lighting in homes or cities, the dark hours of the night could be times of danger and vulnerability. For any size-able community, it was common to employ night watchmen who functioned as a kind of early police force, patrolling the streets to maintain order, and keeping watch over the sleeping inhabitants of the city.

In times of conflict, the role of the night watchman is especially important. Military camps assign sentry duties throughout the night and day, maintaining a high level of vigilance for the protection of active personnel. We can imagine how the lonely boredom of pacing back and forth through the slow watches of the night is interrupted by sudden anxiety, as each small creak and cry is amplified in the stillness of the nocturnal air.

It is not surprising that biblical writers drew upon the image of the watchman's night-time vigil as a vivid metaphor of waiting in prayer. Psalm 130 describes the deep longing of a soul who cries out for God's merciful attention.

> I wait for the LORD, my soul waits,
> and in his word I hope;
> my soul waits for the LORD
> more than watchmen for the morning,
> more than watchmen for the morning. (Psalm 130.5–6, RSV)

The rhythmic repetition of the final phrase evokes something of the effort and intention of keeping awake to sustain a hopeful vigil while others sleep. What keeps the psalmist going throughout his weary prayer is the quiet conviction that dawn will surely come.

In another psalm, we find the striking picture of God himself as the night watchman, who patiently protects his people from danger.

He who keeps Israel will neither slumber nor sleep.
The LORD is your keeper;
the LORD is your shade at your right hand.
The sun shall not strike you by day,
nor the moon by night. (Psalm 121.4–6)

Just as earlier societies divided up the day and night into set duty periods of watch, so it became natural for religious communities to schedule times of prayer according to a similar rhythm and shape. Our Christian canonical hours were developed from earlier Jewish practices which established the pattern of faithful regular prayer times commended by the psalmist who wrote, 'seven times a day I praise you', and 'at midnight I rise to praise you' (Psalm 119.164, 62).

The night watch became one of the distinctive disciplines of the Christian monastic movement, dating back to the days of the fifth-century desert fathers and mothers who rose before dawn to greet each day with prayer. These early Christians wanted to meet the Lord when he came again 'in the evening, or at midnight, or at cockcrow, or at dawn' (Mark 13.35). Monks and nuns saw themselves as sentinels on the ramparts, keeping watch on behalf of the whole church for the fulfilment of God's promise (cf. Isaiah 21.8; 62.6–7).

Right down to the present day, monks and nuns in religious communities offer their pre-dawn office of Vigils, lifting up the hours of the night in prayer to God, and invoking a spirit of expectancy for the coming day. The night watch then continues in contemplative silence from the conclusion of Vigils until the morning prayer of Lauds. These quiet hours before dawn foster a unique stillness, waiting in hushed anticipation, as lovers wait upon the return of the beloved.

This sense of loving adoration is beautifully captured by Chiara Lubich, foundress of the Focolare Movement, who wrote: 'Only love is watchful. This is a characteristic of love. When one loves a person, one watches and waits on him unceasingly. Every moment spent away from the loved one is lived with him in mind, is spent waiting. Christ asks for love, so he requires us to watch' (Lubich, p. 37).

The practice of compassion

> Keep watch, dear Lord, with those who wake, or watch, or weep this night,
> and give your angels charge over those who sleep.
> Tend your sick ones, Lord Christ, rest your weary ones,
> bless your dying ones, soothe your suffering ones,
> pity your afflicted ones, shield your joyous ones;
> and all for your love's sake.

As a hospital chaplain, I spend many hours by day and night with those keeping vigil at the end of a loved one's life. This tender prayer by St Augustine of Hippo is one of the most ancient texts that I love to share with families. When I am called to the bedside on these occasions, it is a privilege, not only to commend the dying soul, but also to minister to those gathered around them in solidarity and support. Often, I will give them a prayer card with these words to sustain them in their vigil. 'This is for you. It is a very beautiful prayer. You might find comfort in these traditional words to help you through this time.'

Keeping vigil at the end of life is a unique act of compassion. For Christians, it is also a robust act of hope as we wait for the Lord, in his own time, to come and take his loved one to their eternal home. Seeing a room full of chairs around the bed reflects this loving commitment, as friends and family members unite all their faith and hope and love to keep watch for that final hour.

Sometimes it is very clear that death is approaching soon, and that a person wants his or loved ones to be close at hand. But things are not always so tidy. Dying can be an unpredictable or long drawn-out affair, and it may not be possible to judge the best time to call a family for the final hours. When a vigil drags on from days and nights into weeks, or even months, we need to be realistic about the cost of caring so intensely and so personally for someone we love. How can we spread the load? Would it be wise to take some time out, and return refreshed? It is not unknown for a dying person to slip away peacefully while their loved ones are out of the room.

In these tender waiting times, there are many graces both to give and to receive. Learning to give practical comfort may involve simple mouth care, soothing massage and careful re-positioning. Perhaps the sound of music or birdsong may be welcome, perhaps some favourite reading or gentle conversation; but, equally, there will be some who prefer quietness in their final hours. It takes thoughtfulness and diplomacy to judge what is more supportive than intrusive. There will be skills to learn in working calmly alongside nurses and doctors, who have a particular role in assessing and relieving troublesome symptoms, or with other carers who take the heavy end of physical support and hands-on hygiene care.

Love and grief bring complex, sometimes shocking, emotions to the surface. It is not unusual to feel fractious and ungrateful, while trying to offer loving companionship to the person who is dying, and to all those whose relationships matter at this time. It is probably an understatement to say that most families are complicated; and, in the intensity of gathering for vigil, long-standing bonds of love can be acted out in ways that hurt as well as heal. Understanding and forgiveness are never more needed than when sibling rivalry, or competitive caring, bedevils our best efforts to show final concern. Perhaps the disciple who struck out with his sword in the garden of Gethsemane (Luke 22.50) stands for any one of us who has lashed out uncontrollably at others because of our own unbearable fear and grief.

All these practical and emotional aspects of human compassion we might helpfully reflect on as we contemplate the passion of Christ. Yet something deeper beckons when we are called to abide amid the fear and chaos, and to walk the last mile along a fellow-pilgrim's journey. At the heart of loving vigil is prayerful presence. This is what Christ begged of his disciples in the garden, what religious communities offer up for the world in their faithful liturgies, and what generations of Christians have been taught to respect as their final labour of love – to bless those who are drawing close to the threshold of heaven.

There can be no right or wrong way to pray at such an awesome time. I have seen countless families take comfort in the gravitas of traditional prayers such as Psalm 23, 'The Lord is my shepherd', or the rosary, or the magnificent *Proficiscere*, 'Go forth on your journey, Christian soul'. Some look to classic texts from literature, the ever-poignant prayer from *Hamlet* speaking for many: 'May flights of angels sing thee to thy rest' (Act 5, Scene ii). Others choose more homespun words for keeping watch: perhaps a simple one-line prayer – 'Bless us in our sorrow; uphold us in our pain' – or the heartfelt outpouring of a very personal 'thank you, and goodbye'.

Words that try to contain the bitterness and the dread, as well as the hope and love and unutterable mystery, are part of the practice of a rich and generous compassion, as we wait and watch together. Sometimes it can be the essential role of a minister, as poet Anne Stevenson explained, 'to take care of the words' (Stevenson, p. 62). Our own best attempts will often feel trite and inadequate. More importantly, beneath and between the flow of words, we offer the outpouring of a deeper soulfulness, which comes from a still centre of loving contemplation.

The practice of contemplation

Waiting for death may be the ultimate school of godly patience, especially when the time of release is long delayed. For those who watch, and for the one who walks the final steps of their pilgrim journey, the patience to endure will require every ounce of faith and hope and Christian love. My aim throughout this book is to help us rehearse those practices of patience that can sustain and sanctify us throughout life and, ultimately, in the hour of our death. One of the most essential of these practices is the spiritual practice of contemplation.

Contemplation has been helpfully described as a long, loving look at the real (Burghardt, p. 89). It is a practice fundamental to the monastic paradigm of watchful prayer; and yet, in its sheer simplicity, the practice of contemplation is something that can be embraced by any Christian in any circumstance. It is exquisitely suited to the context of a loving vigil, where deep calls to deep at the final shore edge of bodily life. Alone or with others, we commit to watch and pray as earthly life gives way to death.

There is no systematic way of describing contemplation. It is a discipline that is learned and understood from within, whenever we give ourselves to gaze upon the world before us with genuine love. There is an inherent patience in the practice of contemplation. As we slow down our anxious thoughts, opening our hearts to a deeper presence, we begin, by some primal instinct of the soul, to shift the frame of consciousness from our hurried and fearful earth-bound preoccupations towards the spaciousness and the endless mercy of God.

Keeping vigil with the dying is like watching the slow turn of the tide. At Crosby Beach, near Liverpool, Antony Gormley has created a marvellously evocative representation of our undefended humanity in his installation of one hundred 'iron men'.[1] Walking among these life-sized figures as they stare out towards the sea is a deeply absorbing experience. Around them, the sands and shifting waters come and go, through periods of utter exposure to times of terrifying submersion. All the while, pitted against the elements, each naked figure stands gazing outwards to an unknowable horizon. What is it to live? Some bear the indignities of perching seagulls, or the mocking festooned remnants of football scarves or Santa suits left by adolescent partygoers. What is it to die? One by one, the outermost figures fade from view beneath the advancing tide. What is it to face forward? What is it to be human? What is it to hold faith?

Contemplative questions arise naturally enough at the extremities of life. But to cultivate a contemplative spirit we need to rehearse some kind of spiritual practice in everyday life, learning to open the eyes of our heart to the unfathomable wonder of God's loving presence in the entirety of our living and dying. Ours is a culture that has flattened out much of its spiritual imagination, and it takes practice to train our hearts to gaze inwardly and outwardly with the patient expectancy of a contemplative soul.

The spiritual exercises offered in this book illustrate some of the practices that can help to develop our innate capacity for contemplation. This is not so much a seeking for mystical experiences for their own sake, as a readiness to appreciate, and become more consciously aware of, God's intimate and loving activity in every part of our lives. Exploring the presence of God in this way enables us to see and shape reality from a very different perspective. Through acts of loving and watchful attention, our vision becomes gradually aligned with the mysterious movement of God's unfolding purposes, even in situations of immense suffering and strain.

Without contemplation, we are tempted to hopeless impatience, often making ourselves and those around us thoroughly miserable. The problem of impatience in those who are sick and dying has long been recognized as a spiritual issue. Dating back to the fifteenth century, the pious texts known as *Ars Moriendi* expounded an art of dying for faithful Christians. Among a wealth of practical and spiritual advice, they present a candid assessment of the prevailing temptations for the soul approaching death; and, interestingly, the chief temptation – along with lack of faith, despair, vanity and greed – is the temptation to impatience. Some of the classic versions of the *Ars Moriendi* are accompanied by wonderful woodcuts. I love the humorous illustration of impatience that depicts with cartoon clarity the ill temper of a dying man who is lashing out at everything and everyone, including a remarkably vigorous kick in the chest to his attending physician!

Perhaps one modern expression of this angry impatience in the face of suffering is the cry for assisted suicide. It is understandable, in many ways, that the slow approach of death can tempt people to anxiety and despair; and that, for those used to retaining control over their lives, their impatience may find expression in a desire, if not to kick their physician in the chest, then, perhaps vociferously, to demand release from their suffering.

It would be very hard-hearted not to recognize the genuine concern and compassion that motivates friends and family members to seek an end to their loved one's suffering by considering an end to their life, and there are many arguments that can be rehearsed both in favour of and against euthanasia or assisted suicide. It is not the purpose of this book to resolve this enormous moral and social debate. From many years of caring for individuals and families in the course of terminal disease, I would simply observe that a watchful, loving and contemplative attitude, even in the face of intractable pain and distress, can bring about remarkable transformations. Where there is time and awareness, much spiritual growth can take place. The decision to embrace the grace of waiting invites a 'long, loving look' at the realities of a whole lifespan, including its bitter and painful aspects, in a way that can be deeply healing and full of consolation.

The gift of consolation

There is a priceless gift for those who plumb the depths of watching and waiting. It is a gift of overwhelming consolation: God will not leave his children 'comfortless'.

Jesus' powerful farewell discourse in the fourth gospel is rich with consolation for all who watch and wait, sorrowing. Modern translators may find no warrant for the Authorized Version's translation of the word for his bereft disciples as 'comfortless' (John 14.18, AV), with its apparent connection with the promise of the coming 'Comforter' (John 14.16, AV). (A more literal translation (NRSV) has the disciples 'orphaned', and awaiting the coming 'Advocate'.) But, as so often, the older translators had an instinct for the emotional and spiritual depth of a text that sometimes eludes those more concerned with linguistic exactitude.

Giving 'comfort' is what parents do for small children when they are troubled and afraid. We speak in homely ways of giving a 'comforter' to an infant who is frightened of being left alone. The soft toys and comfort blankets familiar to family life are described in psychological terms as 'transitional objects'. They afford a point of intimate connection with a larger symbolic world, channelling the strength and consolation of the parent's more immediate presence to the one who is feeling bereft.

The gift of consolation, or 'comfort', is the fruit of faithful, caring relationships. It is felt most keenly when those relationships are tested to the point of breaking. This is the paradox underlying Jesus' teaching: 'Blessed are those who mourn, for they will be comforted' (Matthew 5.4). We can see the reality of Christian consolation being proved and tested in the lives of the early disciples following Jesus' death. And in the teaching of St Paul, we find a very powerful description of its patient outworking through times of affliction.

> Blessed be the God and Father of our Lord Jesus Christ, the Father of mercies and the God of all consolation, who consoles us in all our affliction, so that we may be able to console those who are in any affliction with the consolation with which we ourselves are consoled by God. For just as the sufferings of Christ are abundant for us, so also our consolation is abundant through Christ. If we are being afflicted, it is for your consolation and salvation; if we are being consoled, it is for your consolation, which you experience when you patiently endure the same sufferings that we are also suffering. (2 Corinthians 1.3–6)

Several aspects of Christian consolation stand out in this passage. First, the reality of this consolation is grounded in the inexhaustible mercy of God. Like the child who finds comfort in the symbolic representation of parental love, the Christian finds real and genuine consolation in a filial relationship with 'the Father of all mercies and God of all consolation' whose goodness and care is a matter of deep and proven trust. Second, the gift of consolation is a response to severe and extended human distress – what St Paul describes as 'affliction'.[2] Arising from the abundant sufferings of Christ himself, the man of sorrows, there is nothing shallow or sentimental about Christian consolation. This is not a trite 'there, there', a superficial balm to soothe trivial anxieties, but a profound 'I will be with you', giving strength to those who patiently endure. The third and important mark of Christian consolation is that its genuineness is proved when it moves the sufferer to a place of greater maturity and generosity, such that they are enabled, like St Paul, to bring consolation to others.

For Christians, the gift of consolation is personified in Christ himself, in his birth and incarnation, in his life and ministry, in his suffering and death, and in his continuing risen presence through the Spirit in the life of the church. This supremely personal gift is summed up in the marvellous messianic title found in St Luke's gospel, where Christ is described as 'the consolation of Israel' (Luke 2.25). It is a phrase that nestles in the delightful story of Simeon and Anna, two ancient and devout servants of God who are found 'watching and waiting' in a decades-long vigil of faithful prayer.

We often recall the story of Simeon and Anna in the season of Advent, when we join them in waiting for the coming of the Messiah. They represent the whole people of Israel who, throughout their history, had known great affliction. They had suffered under slavery in Egypt, tasted bitter conquest and exile, and the ongoing indignity of seeing their Promised Land overrun by foreign powers. They were a people desperately in need of consolation. Simeon had spent his whole adult life watching and waiting for the day of Christ's consolation, and it was given to him to see the promise of God fulfilled. Like a faithful sentry finally discharged from his tour of duty on the ramparts, he could pray as the child Jesus lay in his arms, 'Lord, now you let your servant go in peace' (see Luke 2.29).

In this chapter, we have trodden holy ground alongside some of the greatest saints and exemplars of watchful waiting, drawing strength and encouragement for our own long vigils of sorrowing and grief. Learning from them the grace of patience, our calling is to put into practice smaller and larger deeds of compassion, while cultivating a quiet and contemplative spirit, until God's promised day of consolation finally dawns.

Practicum – watching in love

There is a beautiful story that was often repeated by St John Vianney, a priest in the parish of Ars in France. He noted the example of a villager called Louis Caffangeon who was frequently to be found in the church. Louis was a farmer who would leave his hoe outside the church then go inside to sit in silent adoration, sometimes for hours on end. One day, the priest asked him what he was doing all this time. The man replied, 'I look at the Good Lord, and the Good Lord looks at me.'

Taking time to watch in love before the Lord is one of the simplest and purest spiritual exercises for anyone. It is a practice of genuine contemplation in which our only agenda is to love and to be loved by God. St John Vianney described the lifting up of our heart to the heart of God as like the flame of two candles that slowly melt, to merge, and come to burn as one.

In a slightly different analogy, Rowan Williams once brilliantly described the process of prayer as like sunbathing, something that happens simply by lying there. 'You give the time, and that's it. All you have to do is turn up. And then things change, at their own pace. You simply have to be there where the light can get at you' (Williams, 2005).

Taking time, day by day, for silent contemplation before the Lord is the best spiritual preparation for the practice of patient watchfulness in daily life, moulding and directing our hearts for those times when the deepest reserves of compassion will be asked of us.

In classic monastic spirituality, this posture of contemplative watchfulness is mirrored by an inner vigilance. Soaking up the love of God, morning, noon and night, sustains us for the necessary ongoing discipline of cleansing and renewing our interior life. This is sometimes described in terms of 'watchfulness' of the mind, taking care over the healthy direction of our thoughts, or as a 'custody' of the heart, practising discernment over the use of the emotions. The essential aspect of this lifelong, disciplined practice is that it should be rooted and grounded in prayerful experience of the love of God.

In all the spiritual exercises recommended in this book, the aim is to rehearse a pattern of holy waiting that will sustain you when you come to face more searching challenges in life.

Take some time today, and find a place to be quiet and still, watching with the Lord, with no other agenda than to receive, and return, the sunshine of God's love, which is poured out end-lessly for you and for the whole world.

We wait for thy loving-kindness, O God, In the midst of thy holy temple. (Psalm 48.8, BCP)

Notes

1 Antony Gormley's *Another Place* was installed at Crosby beach in 1997. Each life-sized figure was created from a body cast of the sculptor, permanently mounted on a concrete plinth in the sand where it would test the stillness and movement, time and tide, at the margins of land and sea.

2 See Chapter 5 (The Wine Press), above, for more discussion of St Paul's use of this term.

6

The Winter

Out of the depths I cry to you, O LORD. (Psalm 130.1)

Jack calls into the hospital once a week for lunch in the restaurant. He says that it gives him a convenient break on the way to the supermarket. But usually he takes time to stop by at the chapel, or the clinic, or the ward where Shirley was a patient. When she died six months ago, Jack's whole world was turned upside down, and he still looks for understanding and reassurance in the places where they spent so much of her last months together.

Times of loss and bereavement can be some of the darkest seasons of life, when much that we have loved and cherished goes underground, and we face a long, lonely winter of grieving.

There are shifting seasons in every life. Many of us relish the springtime, when fresh buds awaken and new shoots spring up from the earth, while the world is filled with a sweet sense of expectation. Summer brings warmth, relaxation and happiness, with fresh colour and abundant life. Then comes the autumn, with its gentle hues and luscious fruitfulness. But always we face the slow return to winter, with its hard, cold months of quiet waiting.

These cycles of nature find their inevitable parallels in the life of the soul. We are thrust into seasons of cold and darkness which will not be rushed – times of bereavement and sorrow, periods of inertia or incomprehensible delay. The force of circumstances, or the dark chemistry of the mind, conspires to put life as we have known it on hold. And until this bleak season passes, the soul has little choice but to trust, to endure and to wait.

Knowing ourselves to be creatures of nature in this regard can be a real help and consolation for our spiritual winters of waiting and grief. With or without religious faith, many people feel an instinctive connection with the deep natural order of things. In language that is as painful as it is poetic, many grieving souls turn to the image of winter to express their hollowness and pain.

Over the years, I have often reached for an anthology of poems that was produced by Cruse Bereavement Care in 1984 (Whitaker). The editors compiled a wonderful selection of pieces that help to 'give sorrow words' (*Macbeth*, Act 4, Scene iii) through the slow and beautiful ways in which they articulate the pains of grief. In many of the poems there are echoes of wintertime, 'when all is hollow and the grey clouds mock the sun' (Torrie, p. 91). Dark words and earthy metaphors of the dead husk, the dull clay, the heavy skies and the chill silence resonate with bitter-sweet familiarity for people who are tracing their own weary path through the aching winter of grief.

Poetry can be deeply healing. The words and rhythms of a sensitively written poem help to slow down, and to soothe, our troubled minds. Their symbolic richness bestows a dignity, a rootedness, and a pattern of meaning for the broken fragments of a life that is for ever changed. And, without forcing the pace, the calm patience of a poem can also point forward to the return of a springtime, when, in Keats' hopeful words:

. . . yes, in spite of all,
Some shape of beauty moves away the pall
From our dark spirits. (Keats, p. 51)

The harvest is past, the summer is ended

Winter is a time where nature's life is stripped down. Whether we have lost a loved one through death, or are facing the curtailment of our own life through changing circumstances or health anxieties, we are forced to come to terms with the reality of a loss beyond repair. The bare chill and yearning of grief has something to do with this intimate sense of diminution. Like an amputation, something vital is missing; we feel an empty void where once we had known satisfaction and strength.

Each small detail of life bears the echoes of this loss and hollowness. The empty diary of the unemployed, the vacant chair of the bereaved, the lonely hearth of the abandoned. The sunny days are behind us, and we grieve for the loss of cheer and brightness, and the easy normality of former times. It is a cliché to say that life will never be the same again; but the sheer rawness of grief, and all its crazy contours, expose the extent to which the life that we once knew has been irretrievably undone.

This season of diminishment is a time for patience, as long days and months drag by in a hungry weight of waiting. How long must we bear this awfulness of grief: its heartbreak and weariness? How long before we can start a new day without those sharp pangs of mourning and loss? How long before we can rebuild, and look forward? How long before life begins to feel normal again, or happy, or simply tranquil and hopeful once more?

All those who have journeyed on the road of grief know it to be a slow process without shortcuts. There is no road back, and no way around the chill winds of loss. What is painfully true in experience is that we will have to battle our way through the icy blasts, and to find some way to go on living. Above all, perhaps, we have to be patient.

Let it be cold

The wisdom and resilience of nature can be an inspiration in this process. We human beings belong to a deeper and much larger ecology, which bears witness to an indefatigable hope. As we learn to wait in patience, we may come to appreciate how nature's cold and wintry times are essential to let what is tired and rotten die back, so that one day new life may emerge.

The world of nature teaches us that many plants need a period of cold weather for their flowers to bloom healthily in the spring. Gardeners know that cold snaps are necessary to kill off some of the nastier bugs and infestations. As human beings, we can learn to embrace these slowed-down seasons of nature with all their latent promise. We recognize the unavoidability of our own waiting, a sense of its dark necessity, even in the cruel losses of winter, which can guide our intuitions towards grace and hope.

I am often struck by this quality of quiet hope, especially in the dignity with which many families and individuals bear their mourning. Glimpses of grace shine through the mists of sorrow: in kindly words of personal affection and respect, in graceful rituals of public remembering and release, in the long inner litanies that labour to sift and preserve much that is beautiful from the past. Meanwhile, we learn how all that was ephemeral must be let go, and allowed to lie forgotten. Through these austere and loving efforts, we give our consent to grief, allowing the winter to do its healthy work. While honouring the past, we embrace the astringent task of purifying the memory and imagination of attachments that could never be expected to last for ever.

And what of those who face the lingering losses and more gradual bereavement that comes from protracted physical or mental decline? There are similar stark challenges as their own long, slow winter of grief descends. In Lisa Genova's gentle book, *Still Alice*, she chronicles the relentless descent of Alice Howland, a linguistics professor at Harvard, into dementia. There are icy episodes of terrible distress. How can Alice and her family bear to accept this irretrievable breakdown of memory and mind? At one point in the book we overhear a poignant conversation between Alice and her daughter about the question of whether their love can possibly endure.

'You're so beautiful,' said Alice. 'I'm afraid of looking at you and not knowing who you are.'

'I think that even if you don't know who I am someday, you'll still know that I love you.'

'What if I see you, and I don't know that you're my daughter, and I don't know that you love me?'

'Then I'll tell you that I do, and you'll believe me.'

Alice liked that. (Genova, pp. 257f.)

Such are the patient, loving austerities of the soul's wintertime. Whether we face the inexorable degeneration of Alzheimer's or the ultimate darkness of death, our challenge is to bend all our faith and hope and love to believe that life, though it must be changed, will not finally be taken away. It is a hard, spiritual labour of anticipation and grief.

Psychologists have produced a great deal of research about the detailed emotional and social tasks of mourning. The concept of 'grief work' reminds us of the toilsome re-working of older habits of heart and mind that has to take place, as bereaved people learn to adjust to the deep transformations consequent upon their loss. For spiritual writers, there are larger perspectives and even richer possibilities. Through our tears and sighs, we speak in the language of transcendence, to invoke the dark mysteries of waiting on a living God.

The greatest mystics and poets are those whose words can guide our way into these dry and wintry seasons, where we can 'be still and wait without hope' (Eliot, p. 200). A true spiritual guide knows from experience what it means to dig deep into the ascetic dimensions of the soul, where naked faith and hope and love survive through prayer and patience alone. This is the ultimate 'meaning in the waiting' (Thomas, p. 199) for anyone who believes; and these are the austere, but essential foundations that underpin the practices of waiting we will explore in this chapter.

Learning to wait in the soul's winter requires us to be still at heart, and to trust simply in God, even as we fear that all else is lost to us. Patient of God's promise to be our refuge and inner strength, we embrace the cold, while, in this awful chill of waiting, a kind of numbness settles on the soul. When life itself, cocooned deep within the snows, seems to hang by a thread, we learn what it means to go on waiting, until the silent mystery of new life begins once more to unfold: slowly, darkly and without drama. This is winter patience.

The practice of rootedness

I love to walk through woodlands in wintertime. The great trees, wordless in their wisdom, understand all that is necessary for survival. Stretching out stripped branches, dark against the skies, they bear silent testimony to a patience that rests deep-rooted in the soil. This quality of rootedness is something that I have learned to admire in all truly patient souls.

Unlike the trees of the forest, human beings must consciously resolve how to withstand adversity. We are free to choose whether to practise patience, or not; whether to put down deeper roots, or to thrash around on the surface of things. As people who are grounded in a great tradition, Christians are blessed with every encouragement of teaching and example to invest in a deep-rooted holy patience.

We make it a practice of patience whenever we consciously reach down for the roots of this rich faith tradition. Like a tree in hard times, we trust the instinct that delves deeper into the soil of God's grace. This decision for patience can be easily misunderstood. A tree that withdraws its energies below the ground may look inert, like something lifeless and defeated. Yet if we could see what is going on beneath the surface, we should be astonished at the vast and sophisticated system of nourishment, storage and strength, which sustains a whole industry of survival deep below the external weather of frost, wind and hailstorm.

Something of the same elemental security sustains faithful souls through times of apparent failure and loss. It was well described by the words of Jesus in an older translation of Luke's gospel, 'in your patience possess ye your souls' (Luke 21.19, AV). This kind of self-possession is about the ability to draw inward against all external misfortune, holding on in faith to the greater hope in which our spiritual lives are embedded. It is being anchored in a larger obedience, keeping tryst with a hidden covenant, standing firm on the eternal rock.

This calmness of soul is a characteristic of individuals and communities that have been driven underground by persecution: and perhaps this was the situation envisaged in Luke's gospel. While it is unclear which specific historical onslaught the evangelist was contemplating, his vivid descriptions of political, religious and even cosmic upheaval suggest an event of apocalyptic proportions (Luke 21.9–11). Whatever fearful uncertainties these early believers confronted, they drew their anchoring security from the far greater certainty of the love of Christ. Our own circumstances may be less dramatic, but the durability of our faith through times of confusion and loss demands a comparable deep-rooted patience.

Cultivating these deep roots of patience helps us to draw from unfailing spiritual springs. The psalmist paints a wonderful picture of the tree 'planted by streams of water' which has all the sustenance it needs to resist attrition, and to bring forth its fruit in due season (Psalm 1.3). There is a helpful realism about such imagery, which recognizes both the seasonality of good and bad times, and the abiding faithfulness of a *Deus absconditus* (hidden God), whose mercies may be inscrutable to our blinkered human timeframes of comprehension.

The practice of resilience

Blasted by gale-force winds, and battered by rain and blizzards, a tree in winter needs resilience as well as rootedness if it is to survive extreme climatic stress.

When human beings are similarly overwhelmed by tsunamis of grief and disappointment, they need to draw on those inner resources of dynamic resilience, which are described by poet Marjorie Pizer as like 'weaving bands of steel' into her soul (Pizer, p. 41). For human beings, this is a choice. Faced with adversity, we are free to decide whether and how to keep faith. Our decision to withstand the blasts of winter both requires and reinforces an inner spiritual resilience. Like a tree tossed back and forth by the storms of life, we learn what it means to bend, but not to break.

The root meaning of resilience lies in this quality. Literally, the word 'resilience' describes a capacity to bounce back from disappointment or affliction. In the context of waiting, it reflects our ability to ride the tidal waves of questioning, bewilderment and pain with the composure of faith. Like the resilience of an athlete, which is enhanced through training, there is a quality of spiritual resilience that can be deepened through the determined practices of active patience.

Marjorie Pizer's poem on 'Strength', which was forged in the crucible of her personal experience of grief, points to some of the essential elements in this kind of hardy resilience. First, there is an ascetic determination to make faith-sense out of painful experience. Refusing any denial, she makes a conscious decision to embrace this opportunity to become a stronger person, fully aware that this tempering of her character will take time. Second, she applies herself to both inner and outer resilience. It is not just a matter of putting on a brave face, like some brittle carapace or suit of armour that merely gives an impression of being unperturbed. Of course, we do need a degree of external hardiness if we are to endure the icy blasts of tough times; but Pizer wisely emphasizes the internal disciplines by which we work to exercise the sinews of mind and soul – in all 'the warp and weft' of exhaustion and dogged endurance (Pizer, p. 41).

Up to this point in her poem, we might reckon that all that is necessary is Stoicism, the self-containment and fortitude to endure and to gain some profit from adversity. But something far richer and more mutual emerges later in the poem, where Pizer hints at a faith that links and binds her with the 'bonds of psalms and songs of all who have suffered' (Pizer, p. 41).

It is a telling image for someone who has never been an avowed Christian. Yet the poet's instinctive awareness of a deeper fellowship of suffering shines through at this point. Through the tender mercy of God, and in sweet communion with all the saints, none of us need ever bear adversity alone. Most mysteriously of all, it is precisely in the place of suffering where we are likely to encounter the closeness of Christ, whose wounds are united with every human being who has learned to 'knit stitches of suffering' into outstretched hands (Pizer, p. 41).

One of the research findings in studies of resilience is that the making of shared meaning in adversity emerges as a strong factor for a positive outcome (Smith et al., pp. 437–54). Typically, people who belong to a religious community find spiritual, as well as psychological and social, resources to sustain them through harsh winters of grief. In the great story of Judeo-Christian faith, we have many examples of strong and resilient waiting through periods of adversity. I think of the great prophets, guiding God's people through dark days of exile, instability and fear; or the psalmists who sustained a spirit of devotion through periods of intense uncertainty and upheaval. Perhaps it is not surprising, therefore, that their words on waiting should continue to be a source of strength down the centuries, forging faith-meaning out of some of the most hard-going winters of private and individual, or public and political, tribulation.

'Those who wait for the LORD shall renew their strength,' wrote the great prophet-poet of Jewish exile (Isaiah 40.31). The book of Isaiah is so full of encouragement that it is sometimes referred to as the 'fifth gospel', commending a hopeful, forward perspective for people caught up in the slow, painful outworkings of a difficult history. This future orientation was clearly influential on the ministry of Jesus and the teaching of the early church, and it has left an indelible imprint of hopefulness on all subsequent generations. The Hebrew verb for waiting, *qawah*, describes the essence of confident, expectant faith that cleaves to and waits *upon* God without needing to know precisely what outcome is being waited *for*.

A similarly tireless sense of attachment undergirds the prayers of the psalmist. 'Wait for the LORD; be strong, and let your heart take courage; wait for the LORD' (Psalm 27.14). Again, the verb *qawah* suggests the sinewy cords of connection by which the waiting soul cleaves to God. The etymology of the verb echoes a primitive root word for tying or binding ropes together – a graphic image for the resilient bond of covenant that God promises to his faithful people.

Resilient faith is not a backward-looking or static affair. Rather, it is an active practice of ongoing grappling with God that lays hold of all the strength, hope and courage of a living relationships. One way of seeing this is as an active binding together of past memories of God's faithfulness with a future expectation of God's deliverance. The result is enduring strength for the present and renewed energy for the future: 'They shall mount up with wings like eagles, they shall run and not be weary, they shall walk and not faint' (Isaiah 40.31).

The gift of renewal

Earlier this year, I spent time getting to know Angela. She had suffered a rare neurological complication of a simple viral infection which caused her to lose muscular power in her arms and legs. For months, she battled with paralysis and weakness, never knowing how long her disabling condition might continue.

At last the day came when her strength began to return, and Angela was able to venture out once more with family and friends. Just then, tragically, a second infection compounded the earlier damage and she was paralysed once again, this time even more seriously. At that point, there was nothing for her to do but wait.

I visited her throughout this period, sharing the burden of anxiety and loss, and praying with her for patience and peace. None of us could know when, or even whether, full physical healing might come. But throughout her illness, Angela kept her heart open to a remarkable hope that real spiritual renewal would come to birth through this time of waiting.

The practice of patience is necessarily a long game. During the wintry seasons of life, we need to be intentional about deepening our roots, and learning a new suppleness, if we are to stay resilient and strong. The biological metaphor of traversing a natural cycle of the seasons holds out the promise of hope, with the encouragement that somewhere, in God's future, there is a newness of life that awaits us.

We cannot avoid the darker note, however, in the teaching of Jesus, which reminds us that new life will not come unless we first embrace a kind of death. 'Unless a grain of wheat falls into the earth and dies, it remains a single grain; but if it dies, it bears much fruit' (John 12.24). The entire paschal mystery is compressed in this brief and challenging parable of the natural world.

What I saw in Angela's suffering was a slow miracle of transformation as, very gracefully, she embraced the 'death' of her former healthy persona, as wife and mother, professional and academic. Engaging the dark winter of her paralysis, she matured into a profoundly courageous person of wisdom, generosity and quiet humour, bringing strength and inspiration to her whole family as they waited for 'normal' life to return.

While I was visiting Angela, we watched together as winter slowly turned into a lovely spring. Through her window, we rejoiced to see how the morning mist rolled back to reveal plump buds and fresh shoots of green, all against a lively chatter of birdsong. From years of experience, we spoke of our trust that, yes, spring was once more in the air. But equally, from years of sober experience, we both understood that the turn of the seasons can never be forced. Always, a measure of patience is required.

God's gift of new life is never ours to command. All we can know for certain, as human beings, is that the future will not be a simple return to the past. For the grain that falls into the earth, death is real. And so, for human beings who embrace dark seasons of winter, like seeds that are buried and lost from sight, we must wait without any guarantee of consolation. Whatever sprouts and grows in the future will be a sacred gift of pure grace.

Meanwhile, we might pause to give thanks for the gains of winter, for its comforts as well as its challenges, its wisdom as well as its weariness. Our frosty days will bring their own spine-tingling beauties. Our long, dark nights will make room for reading and recreation. If this is true for the natural seasons of winter, then we may find the faith to discern those deeper spiritual blessings that are tucked away among the dark clouds of grief.

The Victorian poet Christina Rossetti is famous for her haunting Christmas carol, 'In the bleak mid-winter'. The story of her life was dogged with ill health, both mental and physical; and she knew what it was to endure fearful times of winter, which chill and darken, and strip the soul bare.

It was during one of these long spells of depression, waiting for the return of good health, that she wrote her poem 'A Better Resurrection'. Through the fog of her own inner darkness, she managed to compose this luminous prayer of spiritual renewal.

I have no wit, no words, no tears;
My heart within me like a stone
Is numb'd too much for hopes or fears;
Look right, look left, I dwell alone;
I lift mine eyes, but dimm'd with grief
No everlasting hills I see;
My life is in the falling leaf:
O Jesus, quicken me.

Truly a winter soul, Rossetti exercised the deep rootedness and resilience of a strong Christian faith. Her own human happiness as deeply hidden as the rising sap, she still maintained an unshakeable confidence in God's gift of renewal that would, one day, rise again in her spirit.

> My life is like a faded leaf,
> My harvest dwindled to a husk;
> Truly my life is void and brief
> And tedious in the barren dusk;
> My life is like a frozen thing,
> No bud or greenness can I see:
> Yet rise it shall – the sap of Spring;
> O Jesus, rise in me. (Rossetti, p. 137)

Practicum – light a candle against the darkness

In the days before electricity, people used candles and oil lamps to pierce the darkness of long winter nights. A simple candle flame remains an evocative sign of hope, bringing comfort and a sense of gentle prayer into many painful and difficult situations. As the poetry of the gospel has it, 'The light shines in the darkness, and the darkness did not overcome it' (John 1.5).

Human beings, down the centuries, have practised countless traditions associated with candles, some explicitly religious, but many drawing on deeper pre-Christian instincts. Northern European cultures preserved some of these lovely ancient traditions, gradually developing them for religious and Christian purposes. There is a long-standing custom in Scandinavia, for example, of setting candles around the spokes of a wheel. This dates back to the times when farmers would remove the wheels from their carts and wagons, bringing them inside the home for the quieter winter months. For festive seasons, the wheel would be decorated with bright greenery and lit up with candles: the symbol of a flaming wheel representing the hope of the returning suns of summer. Cultural historians trace the origins of our Advent wreath to this kind of folk tradition.

The practice of lighting a candle remains a beautifully hopeful exercise for many people, and not just religious types. In times of grief and sadness, it gives us something practical to do; and it gathers together in one simple and humble gesture our prayer that light will ultimately triumph over darkness. The candle's gentle flame brings solace in our vulnerability, and its quiet persistence speaks of the enduring power of hope throughout our darkest nights.

As a practical conclusion to this chapter's reflections I invite you to give some time to wait in prayer before a candle. You may wish to pray in silence, or perhaps to support your prayer with a simple chant such as the refrain from the Taizé community.

Dans nos obscurités,
allume le feu qui ne s'éteint jamais.

Within our darkest night,
you kindle the fire that never dies away.

Let your prayer be gentle, hopeful and unhurried. Stay with the warmth of the candle flame. Wait quietly, until you feel something of its quiet radiance rekindling the faith and hope and love of your own innermost being.

7

The Womb

For it was you who formed my inward parts; you knit me
together in my mother's womb. (Psalm 139.13)

If I close my eyes, I can remember some of the times in childhood
when I learned a new word. The words that stand out in my memory may have been a bit tricky to pronounce, or perhaps hard
to understand. I enjoyed learning new words that were quirky,
exotic, intriguing, onomatopoeic. But there were other words that
came tinged with a slight sense of danger: and one of these was
the word 'womb'.

Even now, I can remember some of the feelings of uncertainty
and embarrassment that hovered around this word 'womb'. It
was scarcely a swear word, yet I was never quite sure whether it
was safe to say it out loud. To add to my discomfort, I used to get
it confused with a similarly primitive-sounding old English word,
'wound'.

Etymologically, it seems, I was not far off the mark. Our old
English word for 'womb' is the offspring of an older root word,
common to many languages, which refers to an opening, or hollow, or space in the body. In modern usage, the 'womb' is our
native word for the female uterus; but, as befits a place of immense
fertility, it is often used metaphorically to describe the birthplace
of all manner of new possibilities.

Over the passage of years, that little word 'womb' has grown
and stretched, in my own imagination, to contain many wonders
of meaning. It has also bled and groaned with the travail of much
pain and disappointment. Through the course of my personal and
sexual, as well as pastoral and professional, experience the image
of the womb has become a deep and complex symbol that holds,

like the little town of Bethlehem, 'the hopes and fears of all the years'.

Writing now, as a grown-up, about the meaning and potential enfolded within this little word 'womb', I still hear the echoes of something that sounds rather more like a 'wound'. But within 'the womb of time', as we might say, I have also learned to marvel at one of the most glorious, and terrible, human symbols for the supremely maternal grace of waiting.

The treasures of darkness

There is a kind of waiting that is so full of longing that it hurts. In this chapter, I want to explore this intensely expectant and holy patience that belongs to the deep-seated womb space where our keenest hopes for the future come to their conception and birth.

The maternal womb is a dark and intimate place, made for expectancy. It is where we cherish into being the germ of a new life that is terribly precious, fragile and beautiful beyond words. Full-grown women are familiar with its changing seasons; gawky schoolgirls learn its rollercoaster rhythms; while unborn children bask in its innermost security. Yet the female womb remains a waiting chamber of profound symbolic mystery, charged with biological and sexual, political and mythical, liminality – a visceral hollow where life and love, death and darkness, perilously interweave.

I cannot write of the joyous expectancy of pregnant mothers without recalling the crushing disappointments of women who have lost much hoped-for babies. I dare not contemplate the sweetness of fertility without calculating its fearsome cost. To speak of the eager anticipation of pregnancy is to tread the pendulum edge of human hope, where the birth-pangs of creation play out their fiercest crescendos on frail human flesh.

Most of all, I am hushed before the sheer maternal loveliness of all that is dearly entrusted to the swelling womb: of sacred body and naked soul, of anxious time and boundless eternity. The womb is where every story of human waiting begins: with much yearning and inward patience, and in the dark.

Counting the days

An old friend recently posted a photograph of her newborn baby. He was utterly delightful, a real sweetheart, dressed in a cosy blue bodysuit with the caption across his chest: 'I've just done nine months inside.'

A baby's time from conception to birth averages forty weeks. In that time, there is a huge amount of anatomical and physiological change, and emotional and social adjustment. The slow, gradual ripening of a pregnancy proceeds at a pace that cannot be hurried. Our human gestation period of nine months is as nothing, though, compared to the time taken by other large mammals: horses take eleven months, rhinos fourteen months, sperm whales sixteen months, elephants famously take twenty-two months, while top of the league frilled sharks carry their young for up to three and a half years.

While each expectant mother counts the days, the seed within her womb is growing and developing its own distinctive vitality. There is a necessary sequence to its embryonic development, laid down through long ages of genetic and evolutionary wisdom. The patience of growing things rests in following this steady course of developmental progress, through which there can be no skipping of the intermediate stages. As she counts each passing day, the mother trusts and prays that her precious seed of new life, hidden deep within the womb, will slowly unfold to be a healthy and happy child. Gestation is so much a matter of patience and time.

'Above all, trust in the *slow* work of God,' counselled the Jesuit priest Teilhard de Chardin in one of his wartime letters. He was writing from the muddy quagmire of the trenches to a young cousin, Marguerite, who was struggling to find her way forward in life. Teilhard's advice is as relevant to expectant parents as it is to pastors and politicians, researchers and creative artists, or to young people in search of their vocation. 'We are, quite naturally, impatient in everything to reach the end without delay.' It is hard to live in the liminal space, to be in formation, en route to something unknown, something new. 'And yet it is the law of all progress that it is made by passing through some stages of instability – and that may take a very long time' (de Chardin, p. 57).

Some of the most important things in life take a long time to ripen to maturity. Giving the necessary time to nourish our own souls, to nurture the mental and spiritual resources of others, to incubate the germ of an idea, these are the motherly tasks of many a season of pregnant waiting. Things must unfold and develop, slowly quickening and coming to birth, in their own good time. Our task, like that of a farmer, is to feed and water, and patiently tend, whatever seeds of hope God has planted for an unknown and unimaginable future.

This patient respect for the unperturbable rhythms of life comes across strongly in the nature parables of Jesus, with all their resonances of motherly gentleness and grace. He speaks of seeds growing silently in the good earth, or the leaven that works quietly through the lump of yeasty dough. Nothing is gained by forcing the biologically ordered pace. Grace lies in a patient receptivity, a steady ripening, a willing response to the necessary slowness of good and growing things.

The spiritual subtleties of this respect for unforced patience are beautifully expressed by Søren Kierkegaard. In his perceptive meditation on *Purity of Heart*, Kierkegaard names, with memorable clarity, 'the slowness of the Good' as a characteristic aspect of divine mercy towards our frail humanity. In contrast to the busy human egocentrism that storms about 'noisily and restlessly' in pursuit of some hurried and heroic goal, God, in tender mercy, humbly accepts the temporal limitations of the flesh. In contrast to our impatient human self-assertion, 'the Good puts on the slowness of time as a poor garment, and in keeping with this change of dress one who serves it must be clothed in the insignificant figure of the unprofitable servant'.

Kierkegaard is keenly aware of the ill-temper underlying our busy impatience, the cruelty disguised beneath our self-centred hurry and haste. Distracted and double-minded, the self-important person 'cannot, he will not understand the Good's Slowness; that out of mercy, the Good is slow; that out of love for free persons, it will not use force; that in its wisdom toward the frail ones, it shrinks from any deception'. With devastating accuracy, Kierkegaard pinpoints the root of such a habitual arrogant person: 'He cannot, he will not understand, that the Good can get on without him' (Kierkegaard, pp. 101, 103).

In pregnancy, we may count the days, but there is no way to control their necessary slowness. One of the most sobering things for an expectant mother is the extent to which she is physiologically tamed and confined by this slowness. She can no longer dominate her time, or even her own body. At the most intimate level, as her little one grows and expands within the womb, the mother learns how the slow trajectories of gestation are simply not hers to command. Her experience of pregnancy rewrites all the former rules of time management, as the boundaries of a busy world 'shrink to the parenthesis of the belly' (Menkedick, 2015).

The practice of noticing

For a generation obsessed with productivity and speed, this slow passivity of pregnant waiting can be deeply disconcerting. We are no longer in the driving seat. There is no lordly dictation of successes and outcomes, and no hiding from the implacable slowness of confinement: only an ever deeper physical and psychological immersion in the gathering present, and in the growing womb.

Yet there is equally nothing idle about the slow stretching, swelling and stirrings of a pregnant womb. There is a new kind of tautness and intensity about this gestation time. It becomes a time of all-consuming interiority, wonderful and weighty, as the mother waits upon the secret mystery that is slowly coming to fruition – a child of her own flesh.

Even the most activist personality, during such a time, bends towards the contemplative. Slowly, somewhat shyly, the expectant mother embraces a depth of anticipation, a quality of waiting, which is like no other. 'Although waiting is not *having*, it is also having,' writes Paul Tillich. Aching with the exquisite tension between the already and the not-yet, the maternal womb swells to contain a relationship, and a work in progress, which is already in some sense fully underway.

> The fact that we wait for something shows that in some way we already possess it. Waiting anticipates that which is not yet real. If we wait in hope and patience, the power of that for which

we wait is already effective within us. He who waits in absolute seriousness is already grasped by that for which he waits. He who waits in patience has already the power of that for which he waits. (Tillich, p. 151)

This phenomenal power becomes concrete in the noticing. Remember the thrill of the first flutters of quickening, when a mother feels the wriggling and jiggling of her child in the womb. Or think of the eager attentiveness of the farmer, scanning his fields for the first green shoots of a new harvest – 'first the blade, and then the ear, then the full corn shall appear'. There is a loving, active excitement and sheer delight, which waits on tiptoe-alert for every little sign of the new life waiting to spring forth.

'Behold, I am doing a new thing [says the LORD]; now it springs forth, do you not perceive it?' (Isaiah 43.19, RSV)

This is the practice of noticing, and it infuses our waiting with warmth and parental concern. The mother-to-be is attentive to the smallest of changes. She is noticing, and welcoming, to the first inklings of new life. Peaceful in the present, and hopeful of the future, her practice of noticing gives shape and palpable commitment to the waiting, inciting her to a deeper patience and steadier nurturing of the seed within.

This maternal noticing bears the disposition of an enraptured poet or a besotted lover. It is a gaze, a savouring, a slow recognition and recital of the unique wonders of a world that is slowly coming to birth. It is the way of a mystic, delicate, bitter-sweet and captive to the unfolding promise within. Their noticing entails a willing suspension of impatience, a readiness to dwell more deeply with the slowness and gradual coming-into-being, all for the sake of a richer relationship with the beloved.

Modern mothers, of course, have all the detailed factual measurements of advanced sonography to inform their eager imaginations. There are countless books and websites that chart the growing stages of a 'normal' – that is, statistically normal – pregnancy. At four weeks, your baby is the size of a poppy seed. As early as six weeks, the first signs of a beating heart can be detected. By fourteen weeks, the child can be seen pulling a face or sucking her thumb.

'I praise you, for I am fearfully and wonderfully made,' wrote the psalmist, long before such fine-tuned details of embryology were commonly understood, but not before the deep spirituality of a ripening pregnancy could be experienced as a wonder of grace. 'My frame was not hidden from you when I was being made in secret, intricately woven in the depths of the earth' (Psalm 139.15). In timeless poetry, the psalmist reflects the tender awareness of a God who is intimately concerned with the developing person and their emerging life. It dares to suggest that the slow and loving evolution of a mother's relationship with her baby is held within a larger gaze of eternal love, as God shares and yearns and stoops to notice each tiny detail of the miracle of her unfolding new life.

Of course, there will be long periods of quiescence when there is nothing much to notice beyond the sheer weight of our own waiting. Patience does not always give way to ready miracles. Fidgety days and nights, when the hours hang heavy, are part and parcel of the necessary incubating time for any pregnant mother or creative artist. If we are to notice anything beyond our own frustration at these times, then we shall need to practise the poet's 'negative capability',[1] which bears the hollowed-out wound of the waiting womb with serious courage as well as patience.

In her moving biography, *H is for Hawk*, Helen Macdonald describes a time when she first learned a hard lesson in patience from her father. She was only nine years old when he invited her to join him in a woodland hideout, watching and waiting for a sight of stunning sparrowhawks.

> For a while it had been exciting to stare into the darkness between the trees and the blood-orange and black where the sun slapped crazy-paving shadows across pines. But when you are nine, waiting is hard. I kicked at the base of the fence with my wellingtoned feet. Squirmed and fidgeted. Let out a sigh. Hung off the fence with my fingers. And then my dad looked at me, half exasperated, half amused, and explained something. He explained *patience*. He said it was the most important thing of all to remember, this:

that when you wanted to see something very badly, sometimes you had to stay still, stay in the same place, remember how much you wanted to see it, and be patient. 'When I'm at work, taking photographs for the paper,' he said, 'sometimes I've got to sit in the car for hours to get the picture I want. I can't get up to get a cup of tea or even go to the loo. I just have to be patient. If you want to see hawks you have to be patient too.' He was grave and serious, not annoyed; what he was doing was communicating a grown-up Truth, but I nodded sulkily and stared at the ground. It sounded like a lecture, not advice, and I didn't understand the point of what he was trying to say. (Macdonald, p. 10)

The practice of nourishing

'For the sake of one line of poetry,' confided Rilke, 'one must see many cities, people, and things.' Good writing, he had learned from long experience, is a matter of immense patience. It cannot be dashed off in a hurry. 'One should wait and gather the feelings and flavours of a whole life' (Rilke, p. xii).

This patient gathering of experience, and generous nurturing of the good, is as vital for the creative artist or the project leader or the scientific researcher as it is for the expectant mother. Ideas need feeding. Skills need honing. Relationships need cultivating. Infants need constant, faithful nourishing. In each case the investment in the future is costly, organic and intimately personal.

We know that the female womb is designed for this slow, rich and sustained practice of nourishing. Its internal structure gradually adapts to receive the implanted microscopic embryo that will grow into a tiny foetus, attached by its own umbilical cord to the mother's placenta. Through the cord and the placenta, microscopic blood channels carry ceaseless currents of vital nutrients to feed the embryonic child, sustaining a healthy hormonal and chemical milieu. The mother, for her part, is 'eating for two', aware that the quality of her diet, for good or ill, will impact on the future well-being of her child.

Healthy waiting always requires sustenance of some kind or another. I may be waiting for a clearer discernment of a future vocation; and, as I wait, I foster my talents. If I am waiting for an idea, or a project, to grow and take shape, then, as I wait, I nourish my imagination. If I have to wait for the weariness of ill health, or family tragedy, to ease away, then, as I wait, I replenish my spiritual energies. And when I come to wait for the finality of death to bear my whole life home to God, then, as I wait, I construct a loving legacy.

The image that Jesus gave to his disciples, as part of his final legacy, was of a vine sustaining and connecting its branches (John 15.1–11). As a picture of costly and organic attachment, it holds rich resonances with the intensely personal nourishment that is fed through the umbilical cord to a growing child.

Jesus urges his spiritual offspring to *abide* in him (John 15.4). The Greek verb, *meno*, is directly related to the word for patience, *hypomene*. It has the same connotations of continuity and an abiding relationship. We must *abide* in the vine if we are to gain nourishment and to grow. Jesus promises that through our abiding, and patient waiting, we will bear much fruit (John 15.5).

Organic, and frequently maternal, metaphors proliferate in the developing early Christian spiritual writers. The image of Christ nurturing his children like a mother is prominent in leading teachers from St Anselm to Julian of Norwich. Bernard of Clairvaux's famous treatise on the Song of Solomon speaks warmly and explicitly of the breasts of Christ gently suckling and nourishing his little ones.

In the New Testament we find, somewhat surprisingly, that the apostle Paul often uses maternal imagery to describe his own ministry of teaching and pastoral care, writing of himself as a woman in childbirth, or as a nursing mother (Galatians 4.19; 1 Corinthians 3.1–2; 1 Thessalonians 2.7). So deeply felt was St Paul's maternal affection that when his followers came to meditate on his martyrdom, they described how the executioner's sword drew, not blood, but milk from his wounds (*Acts of Saint Paul* in Gaventa, p. 14); and subsequent generations of pious Christians remembered St Paul as 'our greatest mother' in the faith (Anselm, *Prayers*).

Giving generous time and sacrificial commitment to the nourishing of other people, and oneself, is the perfect opposite to the hurried and distracted temper of our age. In contrast to the persistent open-heartedness of the maternal spirit, we tend to undervalue the slow incubation and measured investment in things of potentially eternal worth. The challenge to our generosity comes when we can see no obvious correlation between nourishing a person or a project and seeing its final outcome. When we glimpse no immediate return on our investment, and not even a hint of any green shoots of new life on the horizon, then the test of our genuine faith and hope and love will lie in our patient determination, in spite of every uncertainty, to go on generously casting our bread upon the waters (Ecclesiastes 11.1).

The gift of naming

'And his name shall be called Wonderful, Counseller, The mighty God, The everlasting Father, The Prince of Peace.' (Isaiah 9.6, AV)

It is a lovely thing, as a priest and a chaplain, to be present for the baptismal blessing of a new child. To watch a mother caressing her child's velvet face, softly gazing into their newborn eyes, is a perennial wonder. In the face of God, with hopefulness and prayer, the parents are invited to 'name this child'.

It is a crowning moment for the patient soul to bestow the gift of a new name. When, in the fullness of time, God brings to birth the child of our longing; when newness of life returns to a weary earth, and fresh signs of harvest spring forth for a hungry people; when a long-drawn-out and difficult project finally comes to completion; then the sign and celebration of a promise fulfilled is to name the gift and pronounce the blessing.

As children, some of our earliest experiences involve coming to know and to name our world. We love to name the things that we relate to, and relish the responsibility of bestowing a name on a doll or a rabbit or a kitten. The name we choose will gather a whole constellation of meanings and memories that reveal the uniqueness of the creature on whom the name is bestowed.

'What's in a name?' teased Juliet, discounting rather casually the shadows of enmity that threatened her love for one of the

Montague clan (*Romeo and Juliet*, Act 2, Scene ii). Ancient societies knew better than to underestimate the power of names, for good or ill; and the gift and responsibility of naming a child was taken with utmost seriousness. Very often, as in many contemporary religious traditions, it was associated with a solemn blessing.

In biblical stories, the gift of a name was sometimes proclaimed by an angel. The patriarchs Ishmael and Isaac, the forerunner John the Baptist, as well as Jesus himself, were endowed with the solemn imprimatur of a heavenly blessing that gathered the power and significance of their role and awesome destiny into a divinely given name (Genesis 16.11; 17.19; Luke 1.13; 1.31).

Thoughtful parents invest time and care in the choice of a name, sometimes waiting for days or even weeks after a birth to seal their decision. A strong name will both affirm and inspire the uniqueness of the personality who is being grafted into the family tree. A good name will do more than describe; it will evoke the spirit of a new life. The gift of naming will carry a long history, and will look forward into a far future, stretching out with the child's soft fingers to embrace unforeseeable sorrows and joys.

To name one's child is to seal our own part in a wonderful act of creation. There are names that just seem to 'fit'. We recognize that 'she's a Lucy' or 'he's a real Oscar', smiling at the resonances that accord so rightly. Perhaps we choose a name that links a child to our family, that honours our past, or that links them with someone we admire. There may be a classic meaning, or totemic significance, which gives depth and wonder to the name. I love the fact that 'Margaret' means a pearl, infusing my own given name with the glorious image of 'the pearl of great price' (Matthew 13.45–46).

To find the 'right' name we try out the sounds, we play with the archetypes and images they evoke, hoping to gather the mystique of a living presence that can enlarge into a brightening future. It is an awesome task to name a child, and it can be dangerous if it is not inscribed with care. We don't have to be hard nominative determinists to appreciate that people grow into the names they have been given; or to chuckle at the ways that our children grow to relate to their dolls or pet animals, just according to the names they themselves have coined for them. From sad experience, we know that the folly of a badly chosen name can blight a person's confidence for decades.

Choosing a name is one of the loveliest gifts of patience: and it takes patience to get it right. This is vitally true when it comes to naming our children and, in lesser measure, it is important for the process of naming our non-human progeny – choosing the title of a book, or finding a strapline that will enhance, rather than cheapen, a project or piece of work in which we have invested our personal reputation and energies.

'The naming of the world, which is an act of creation and re-creation, is not possible if it is not infused with love' (Freire, p. 77). Patiently chosen, and lovingly bestowed, when all our waiting is joyously fulfilled, then the gift of a good name pronounces our richest blessing on the future.

Practicum – a gestation journal

Writing a spiritual journal is a wonderful way of reflecting on our growth and development, our struggles and insights, throughout the pilgrimage of life. Some Christians keep a regular journal as a way of nourishing their spiritual life. Others turn to journalling exercises from time to time as a way of exploring more fully an event or an issue that matters quite deeply to them.

As an exercise to reflect on the material in this chapter, I propose a variation on the well-known model of the 'baby book'. You may wish to write about the spiritual aspects of a pregnancy. Alternatively, whether you are a mother or not, it may be important to think about something else – some kind of commitment or relationship – which you have grown and incubated over a period of time. Either way, you will be able to delve into your own experience to explore the working out of patience over a sustained period of time. You may choose to do this as an ongoing reflection on some current unfolding project, or pregnancy; but for the purposes of distilling your reflections on this book it might be more helpful to look back on a significant time from the past. Either way, the aim is to explore and to practise the grace of waiting.

There is no 'right' or 'wrong' way to go about keeping a journal. Some people choose to write discursively. Others prefer to jot down snippets, or gather pictures, or work out their reflections through creative and visual imagery and expression. Whatever approach seems best to you, the aim of the exercise is to gain fresh perspective, to deepen our awareness, and to listen out for the quiet promptings of God's Spirit in the midst of our lives.

First of all, take some time to decide prayerfully what kind of 'gestation' you will reflect on. Once you have decided, set aside some time – because this is all about our growth and development over time – when you can reflect undisturbed on the experience.

Here are some ideas that might get you started.

- Take a long piece of string, or coloured ribbon, and work it into the shape of your slow gestation. Is it a straight line? Is it curvy and convoluted, or jagged and angular? Is it tangled up in knots?
- Alternatively, sketch out on a page the 'lifeline' of your gestation. What shape will it be? It could be a straight line, or a twisting and spiralling movement across your page. Play with some possibilities until you feel ready to fill out the details.
- If you have artistic or poetic skills, you might decide to create a picture of the womb in words or images.

As the shape of your 'gestation' comes into focus in your mind, reflect prayerfully on the various phases of your experience. Some verses from scripture may point to a deeper significance.

- 'Before I formed you in the womb, I knew you' (Jeremiah 1.5). How did the 'gestation' begin? What were the seeds of new life waiting for conception?
- 'For nothing will be impossible with God' (Luke 1.37). In what ways did you sense God's promised blessing on the unfolding vision? What doubts and questions did you experience?
- 'The child in my womb leapt for joy' (Luke 1.44). What signs of growth and quickening did you notice as the slow incubation took its course? What part did others play in helping you to notice these signs along the way? Were there any important signs that you failed to notice?

- 'Can a woman forget her nursing child, or show no compassion for the child of her womb?' (Isaiah 49.15). What nourishment did you give, and receive, to sustain this long 'gestation'? In what ways have you experienced God's tender compassion and care?
- 'Shall I open the womb and not deliver?' (Isaiah 66.9). How did you relate to God at times of frustration or failure? Was God present for you even when it was hard to keep faith?
- 'We know that the whole creation has been groaning in labour pains until now' (Romans 8.22). When have you felt the piercing pain of the 'wound' in the 'womb'? What has been the cost to you throughout this waiting time, in patience and in suffering? In what ways have others shared in this cost and strain?
- 'He gives the barren woman a home, making her the joyous mother of children. Praise the LORD!' (Psalm 113.9). Is there a sense of wonder and surprise at what has come to birth? Are you able to feel thankful?
- 'The LORD called me before I was born, while I was in my mother's womb he named me' (Isaiah 49.1). Can you name the precious gift that has been conceived, and carried, and brought into the world? What unique blessing will you ask God to impart?

At the end of your journalling, offer an intentional prayer of thanksgiving; and ask God to continue to bless and guide all that has been so patiently brought to birth.

> Let the favour of the Lord our God be upon us,
> and prosper for us the work of our hands –
> O prosper the work of our hands! (Psalm 90.17)

Note

1 The phrase 'negative capability' was coined by John Keats (Letter to G. and T. Keats, 21 December 1817).

8

The God Who Waits for Us

> The Lord is not slow about his promise, as some think of slowness, but is patient with you. (2 Peter 3.9)

A terribly patient figure stands, waiting, at the entrance to the cathedral. We are in Holy Week 2017, and St Paul's Cathedral has invited Mark Wallinger to install his sculpture, *Ecce Homo*, at the top of the west steps for the duration of the Easter season. This life-sized figure of Christ waits, naked and vulnerable, with hands bound behind his back and a crown of barbed wire on his head, for his coming trial, judgement and execution.

Meanwhile, tourists and pilgrims come and go, variously intrigued or oblivious, inspired or amused, some pushing hastily by, while others pause for thought. 'Is it nothing to you, all you who pass by? Look and see . . .' (Lamentations 1.12).

Every now and then, someone will be visibly moved by the image. For a moment, they gaze straight into the face of God, who stands patient and dignified, waiting and utterly vulnerable. And in that haunting moment of recognition, time stands still.

The stature of waiting

Some years ago, W. H. Vanstone produced an influential book, entitled *The Stature of Waiting*. In it, he challenged the idea that human dignity consists in activism and busy outward achievements. Central to his argument was an exposition of how the Christ of the gospels shifts from the active mode of his early ministry into the 'stature' of passive waiting throughout the unfolding drama of his betrayal, arrest, suffering and death.

It was quite shocking in the 1980s to question a traditional doctrine of the impassibility of God. Classic theism taught that to be divine was to live beyond the reach of suffering and pain, viewing the world from some Olympian peak far above the ebb and flow of human passions. Under the influence of Greek thought, many Christian theologians had pictured a God of similar impassibility, who retains his supreme dignity as the 'unmoved mover' of all that he has brought into being.

As Vanstone reread the accounts of Christ's passion, he noted how often the Lord was 'handed over' to wicked men and cruel events. After all the forward momentum and vigorous initiative of the early part of the gospels, when Christ was actively healing and teaching and bringing about tremendous changes, the narrative gear shifts suddenly into a very different kind of atmosphere where Jesus becomes passive and responsive, the one who is 'handed over' to the actions of other people. He is no longer the one who does, but the one who is done to.

For Vanstone, this image of the vulnerable Christ becomes the key to a devastatingly new understanding of divine love and human dignity. God chooses to become passible because of his Love; and in his demonstration of that Love to the uttermost, through the suffering of Christ, he reveals the enormous dignity of the human person, which is not diminished but enriched by the necessities of waiting and the terrible risks of Love.

Longsuffering, and of great mercy

None of this is entirely strange to the scriptural narrative, of course. As far back as the wilderness era, we read of God revealing his character to Moses as the Lord who is 'longsuffering, and of great mercy' (Numbers 14.18; cf. Exodus 34.6, AV). The Hebrew word, *erek*, means 'slow' or 'patient'. And in Greek, the same word is rendered as *makrothymos*, meaning literally 'slow to come to the boil'.

The same beautiful phrase resounds throughout the Old Testament, in psalms (Psalms 103.8; 145.8) and prophets (Joel 2.13; Jonah 4.2; Nahum 1.3), underlining an essential forbearance in God's character and dealings with his people. Out of his own covenant faithfulness, and his deep regard for human frailty, God chooses to show patience and to refrain from destruction and wrath.

In the New Testament, the vision of divine forbearance becomes yet more tender and personal in Jesus' own life and teaching. Jesus' witty parable of the unforgiving servant contrasts the generous mercy of the Lord with his small-minded underling who will not show patience (*makrothymos*) to a fellow-servant (Matthew 18.23–35).

The patient example of Jesus is frequently quoted in the epistles, urging Christians to be long-suffering in their relationships with one another (1 Thessalonians 5.14), and to wait for the outworking of God's assured promises, even in the face of affliction and unjust trials (James 5.7). Their patient long-suffering (*makrothymos*) is counted as one of the gifts of the Spirit (Galatians 5.22), and a primary element of Christian love (1 Corinthians 13.4).

The patient lover

One of the most entertaining books in the Old Testament is the story of an impatient man who projects his own un-forbearing attitude on to his god. Jonah can't wait to see an outbreak of divine vengeance on the people of Ninevah, whom he judges to be disgracefully slow in their response to his preaching. With delicious irony, the unfolding story brings this disgruntled prophet to the reluctant realization that God, who is 'longsuffering, and of great mercy', wants to be just as patient and forbearing towards the people of Ninevah as he has shown himself to be towards his fretful and impatient prophet, Jonah.

The spiritual and psychological insight of this little wisdom tale is priceless. With piercing humour, it gets under the skin of our grumpy impatience with god, life, the universe and everything, showing that the problem is not with God, but with our own egotistic, and ultimately loveless, impatience. We see how laughable we humans are in our sullen, strutting impatience. Just like Jonah, we all want to tell God our plans, and to co-opt his divine energies so that we can get what we want, delivered in our way and according to our timetable.

Nothing could be further from the character of the God who is revealed in scripture, whose only plan and purpose, from all eternity, is the free exchange of Love.

This is the meaning behind God's curious sense of time. It is for Love that 'with the Lord one day is like a thousand years, and a thousand years are like one day' (2 Peter 3.8; cf. Psalm 90.4). God is not a cosmic project planner, driven to achieve a predetermined outcome according to a tightly calculated schedule and deadline. The God whom we meet in the scriptures is never in a hurry; he takes a generous and truly long-suffering approach to the patient outworkings of Love in creation and redemption. And, like every human lover, he is prepared to wait.

Love is the meaning behind some of the beautifully anthropomorphic descriptions of God's patient relationship with the world. In creation, the Spirit broods and hovers over the face of the waters (Genesis 1.2), like a restless mother bird aching to give birth and sustenance to her little offspring. God's primal love affair with his human family unfolds as we read on through the timeless tales of the book of Genesis. At the creation of Adam, God gently moulds the human body, like a careful craftsman working his clay. With the intimacy of a Lover, he breathes out his own spirit-breath to call the inanimate flesh into life (Genesis 2.7). Despite the mistakes and refusals of human love, when the first sinners lose their paradisial home, God clothes and protects them for what will be a harsh world beyond the garden (Genesis 3.21).

God's patient Love shines through the subsequent dark stories of primeval foolishness. When Cain, through envy, is driven to murder his brother, God puts a stop to the cycle of violence by imposing a mark that will protect him from murderous revenge (Genesis 4.15). When human wickedness brings judgement and ecological disaster upon the earth, God's forbearance is demonstrated in his commitment to preserve Noah and to set the rainbow promise of covenant for ever in the clouds (Genesis 9.16). In all the hubris of Babel, God visits an arrogant society with the bewildering consequences of their own faithlessness; but, despite their confusion of languages, God does not deprive them of life and livelihood, but allows them to spread out and populate communities across the face of the earth (Genesis 11.9).

These are the ageless stories of an archetypal God of Love, who cares and strives with feckless humanity, never giving up on his patient determination to call to himself a people who will share his covenant and live out his beautiful dream.

We could go on to unfold the intricate tapestry of God's long-suffering dealings with his people Israel until, in the words of St Paul, 'the fullness of time had come' for him to send his own Son (Galatians 4.4). We could pause with the angel of annunciation, waiting, patient as a suitor, for the 'yes' of Mary's answering love (Luke 1.38). We could watch over the child Jesus, as he slowly 'increased in wisdom and in years' (Luke 2.52), until he was ready to begin his Father's work in public. We could listen to his teaching, sighing deeply with the father who waited for the return of his estranged and embittered children (Luke 15.11–24). We could watch at the foot of the cross, and weep at the garden tomb, and wait with the nervous disciples for the promise of the Holy Spirit.

On every page of the scriptures, we would meet the same patient Lover of souls who yearns and pleads, who seduces and suffers, who rages and ravishes, who labours and cries out, who whispers and agonizes, who burns and bleeds, for Love of the poor human creatures he is drawing to himself. This is the God who, from everlasting to everlasting, is waiting still for us.

The grace of waiting

The tragedy of our impatient generation is that we live as functional atheists, blind and deaf to the loving entreaties of this God who waits eternally for our embrace. Whether it is our shallow hedonism, which demands the immediate gratification of all our egotistical desires, or our self-determined Stoicism, which boasts of its own capacities for endurance and heroic indifference, we resist God's patient invitation to embrace life's necessary waiting as a matter of grace.

Grace is something entirely different: it is a quality of tender relatedness that is suffused with realism, mutuality and gratitude. Our word for 'grace' derives from an old French word for 'kindness'. It bears the echoes of divine mercy and favour, of elegance, good will and virtue. 'Grace has the connotations of a blessing, a quality of the sacred, and implies beauty, ease, and fluidity. Grace seems endlessly responsive to our longing for it' (Dowland Singh, p. 110).

Grace is the beautiful alternative to our ugly and selfish refusals to wait on God. Grace is the conscious choice we make to enter into communion with the loving patience of God, who is eternally creating and re-creating our wonderful world. Grace is the delicate sense of reverence we feel for the gift of a life that we did not manufacture; and grace is the profound sense of respect we owe to the rhythms of an infinitely complex ecology of breathtakingly diverse life-forces that are not ours to command.

Grace is the readiness to embrace, and to be embraced, by a loving providence that will always exceed our limited capacity for comprehension and control. Grace, even in the white heat of terrible waiting, is the peace that passes all understanding. Grace breathes patience, learns wisdom, spreads forgiveness. And grace, within and despite our unfathomable waiting, overflows with a deep and sincere gratitude.

The gift and practice of thankfulness

If there is one practice that both reflects and reinforces the virtue of patience, then it is the habitual practice of thankfulness. The habit of gratitude feeds a perfect virtuous spiral: as we give thanks to God for his grace in our lives, so our habitual enjoyment of his grace is multiplied and deepened. It is for this reason that gratitude is so therapeutic.

In the course of this book, we have identified numerous healthy practices of a deep and growing patience. For the wilderness times, we named the dynamics of necessary surrender and struggle, and the surprising gift of sustenance. In the weary constraints of the wine press, we exercised a commitment to steadfastness and solidarity, and embraced a gift of simplicity. Through the long watch, we urged compassion and contemplation, and uncovered the gift of an answering consolation. In the depths of winter, we worked on rootedness and resilience, while waiting for the gift and promise of renewal. Finally, within the womb of hope, we gave ourselves to the practices of nurture and noticing, in anticipation of the priceless gift of naming and blessing the emergence of new life.

Every one of these practices is enriched through gratitude, as we return the conscious meditation of our heart and mind to the active goodness of the God who is waiting for us. It only takes one moment of gratitude to reset the remorseless self-centredness that, otherwise, can so often embitter our experience of waiting. Instead of a selfish focus on our own miserable constraints and frustrations, a moment of gratitude will raise our awareness of the amazing grace that follows us through all the days of our life.

'Gratitude, praise, hearts lifted high' (Iona Community, p. 43), these are the habits of a eucharistic mind and a eucharistic community that remembers the importance of regular thanksgiving. Whether we practise our gratitude alone or join together in corporate thankfulness with one another, our offering of gratitude pulsates with the grace of a living sacrament, making luminously real and present the mercies of God which we recall. Drawing on the power of memory, this sacrament of gratitude feeds strength into our present struggles, and suffuses all our future worries with loving expectation and quiet hope.

Many years ago, I cared for a West Indian woman by the name of Grace. She was a radiant Christian, and a beautiful witness to the power of God's grace in her life. For several months, Grace wrestled with increasing pain and progressive weakness, as she waited for her cancerous condition to deal the fatal blow. Day by day, as friends and professionals called to help and sustain her, she returned their kindness with astonishing gratitude. She thanked everyone, and she thanked God, always finding new things for which to be grateful, even in the fire of her terminal illness. To visit Grace was nothing less than a conversion experience, as the infectious joy of her thankful heart transfigured the sadness of everyone around her.

Throughout her long illness and difficult life, Grace had learned patience and embraced its rich spiritual gifts with enormous thankfulness. When she died, her pastor confided that there was one verse from the Bible that Grace had insisted should shape the theme for her thanksgiving funeral. It was from Psalm 27.

Wait for the LORD; be strong, and let your heart take courage: wait for the LORD! (Psalm 27.14, ESV)

Practicum – a psalm of gratitude

One final exercise will be a fitting way to conclude this chapter, and to draw together the many gifts and practices of patience that we have been celebrating in this book.

Reading through the psalms of the Bible, we often find patterns of poetry that repeat and reiterate in order to emphasize some vitally important insight or practice of faith. This patient repetition is particularly common in the psalms of gratitude which rehearse the community's memories of all God's faithful acts through history.

As an exercise for your deepening spiritual practice of patience, I invite you to write your own psalm of gratitude. It may be something that you decide to improvise day by day, as you call to mind the particular blessings of the moment. Or perhaps you might write something more enduring, to keep as a regular encouragement to wait for the Lord, and let your heart take courage.

Here is a simple example, based on the pattern of Psalm 136.

O give thanks to the God of the wilderness;
for his patient Love endures for ever.

O give thanks to the God of the wine press;
for his patient Love endures for ever.

O give thanks to the God of the watch;
for his patient Love endures for ever.

O give thanks to the God of the winter;
for his patient Love endures for ever.

O give thanks to the God of the womb;
for his patient Love endures for ever.

O give thanks to the God who waits for us;
for his patient Love endures for ever.

Bibliography

Anselm, 1973, *The Prayers and Meditations of Saint Anselm*, Ward, B. (trans.), London: Penguin.

Arnold, M., 1855, 'Stanzas from the Grande Chartreuse', *Fraser's Magazine* (April 1855).

Brueggemann, W., 2001, *Spirituality of the Psalms*, Minneapolis: Fortress Press.

Burghardt, W., 2008, 'Contemplation: A Long Loving Look at the Real', in Traub, G. W. (ed.), *An Ignatian Spirituality Reader*, Chicago: Loyola Press, pp. 89–98.

Cherry, S., 2012, (online) *Why is busyness so bad?* Available at: http://www.notbusy.co.uk/#why (Accessed 27 April 2017).

Cyprian of Carthage, 'Treatise IX: On Patience', in *The Ante-Nicene Fathers*, Roberts, A. and Donaldson, D. (trans.), 1990, Edinburgh: T&T Clark.

Darling, J., 2015, 'A Waiting Room in August', in Darling, J. and Fuller, C. (eds.), *The Poetry Cure*, Newcastle: Bloodaxe Books, p. 20.

de Chardin, T., 1965, *The Making of a Mind*, London: Collins.

Dowland Singh, K., 1998, *The Grace in Dying*, New York: HarperCollins.

Eliot, T. S., 1963, *East Coker*, in *The Collected Poems 1909–1962*, London: Faber and Faber, pp. 196–204.

Freire, P., 1968, *Pedagogy of the Oppressed*, 30th Anniversary edn, Bergman, M. (trans.), London: Penguin Books.

Gaventa, B. R., 2007, *Our Mother Saint Paul*, Louisville: Westminster John Knox Press.

Genova, L., 2007, *Still Alice*, London: Simon and Schuster.

Harned, D. B., 2015, *Patience: How We Wait Upon the World*, Eugene, OR: Wipf and Stock.

Harvey, A., 1996, *Renewal through Suffering: A Study of 2 Corinthians*, Edinburgh: T&T Clark.

Hesse, H., 1997, *Reflections*, London: Jonathan Cape.

Iona Community, 1989, *A Wee Worship Book*, Glasgow: Wild Goose Publications.

Janouch, G., 1985, *Conversations with Kafka*, London: Quartet Books.

Jones, W. P., 2002, *Teaching the Dead Bird to Sing*, Brewster, MA: Paraclete Press.

Keats, J., 1944, 'Endymion', in *Poems*, London: Everyman, p. 51.

Kierkegaard, S., 1956, *Purity of Heart is to Will One Thing*, Steere, D. (ed.), New York: Harper and Brothers.

Lubich, C., 1974, *Meditations*, New York: New York City Press.

Macdonald, H., 2014, *H is for Hawk*, London: Vintage Books.

MacIntyre, A., 1999, *After Virtue*, London: Duckworth.

McGilchrist, I., 2009, *The Master and his Emissary: The Divided Brain and the Making of the Western World*, New Haven: Yale University Press.

Menkedick, S., 2015, (online) *A Wilderness of Waiting*. Available: http://velamag.com/a-wilderness-of-waiting-2/ (Accessed 8 February 2017).

O'Donohue, J., 2008, 'For the interim time', in *To Bless the Space Between Us*, New York: Doubleday, pp. 119f.

Pieper, J., 1954, *The Four Cardinal Virtues*, New York: Pantheon Books.

Pizer, M., 1992, 'Strength', in *To You the Living*, Pymble, NSW: Collins Angus & Robertson, p. 41.

Reid, A., 1978, 'A lesson in music', in *Weathering*, Edinburgh: Canongate, p. 88.

Rilke, R., 2008, *The Notebooks of Malte Laurids Brigge*, Pike, B. (trans.), Normal, IL: Dalkey Archive Press.

Robinson, J. M., 2015, *Waiting in Christian Traditions: Balancing Ideology and Utopia*, Lanham, MD: Lexington Books.

Rohr, R., *Daily Meditation*, 9 August 2014, Center for Action and Contemplation, Albuquerque, NM.

Rollins, H. E. (ed.), 1958, *The Letters of John Keats*, Cambridge, Cambridge University Press.

Rossetti, C., 1865, 'A Better Resurrection', in *Goblin Market and Other Poems*, London: Macmillan and Co., p. 137.

Schiller, G., 1972, *Iconography of Christian Art*, London: Lund Humphries.

Schnitker, S. A. and Emmons, R. A., 2007, 'Patience as a virtue: Religious and psychological perspectives', in *Research in the Social Scientific Study of Religion*, 18 (2007), pp. 177–207.

Smith, B. W., Ortiz, J. A., et al., 2012, 'Spirituality, Resilience, and Positive Emotions', in Miller, L. J. (ed.), *The Oxford Handbook of Psychology and Spirituality*, Oxford: Oxford University Press, pp. 437–54.

Stevenson, A., 1996, 'The Minister', in *The Collected Poems 1955–1995*, Oxford: Oxford University Press, p. 62.

Thomas, R. S., 1993, 'Kneeling', in *Collected Poems: 1945–1990*, London: Phoenix, p. 199.

Tillich, P., 1953, *The Shaking of the Foundations*, New York: Charles Scribner and Sons.

Torrie, M., 1984, 'The Question', in Whitaker, A. (ed.), *All in the End is Harvest*, London: Darton, Longman and Todd, p. 91.

van Gennep, A., 1960, *The Rites of Passage*, Caffee, M. B. V. and G. L. (trans.), Chicago: University of Chicago Press.

Vanstone, W. H., 1982, *The Stature of Waiting*, London: Darton, Longman and Todd.

Whitaker, A. (ed.), 1984, *All in the End is Harvest*, London: Darton, Longman and Todd.

Williams, R., *Pause for Thought*, BBC Radio 2, 18 October 2005.